PIECE OF MY HEART

A Portrait of
JANIS JOPLIN

PIECE OF MY HEART

A Portrait of
JANIS JOPLIN

by
DAVID DALTON

A DA CAPO PAPERBACK

Library of Congress Cataloging in Publication Data

Dalton, David.
    Piece of my heart: a portrait of Janis Joplin / by David Dalton.
        p.   cm. — (A Da Capo paperback)
    Reprint. Previously published: New York: St. Martins Press, 1985.
    ISBN 0-306-80446-8
    1. Joplin, Janis. 2. Singers — United States — Biography. 3. Rock musicians — United
States — Biography. I. Title.
[ML420.J77D4 1991]   91-19308
782.42166'092 — dc20   CIP

Design by Virginia Rubel
Photo Research by Lynne D. Edelson

Some of the material in this book
originally appeared in substantially different form
in *JANIS* (Stonehill Books/Simon & Schuster, 1971).

This Da Capo Press paperback edition of *Piece of my Heart* is an
unabridged republication of the edition published in New York
in 1985, with the addition of a new introduction by the author.
It is reprinted by arrangement with David Dalton.

Published by Da Capo Press, Inc.
A Subsidiary of Plenum Publishing Corporation
233 Spring Street, New York, N.Y. 10013

Manufactured in the United States of America

To
Susann Dalton and K.
with love

CONTENTS

THE MILLION DOLLAR BASH

◆━━━━◆

A CHRONOLOGY

HOW TO READ THIS BOOK

An Annotated Guide to Our Lady of the Perpetual Party

INTRODUCTION TO THE THIRD EDITION

A couple of Sundays after this book was first published in the fall of 1971, a wicked review appeared in *The New York Times*. "Written with the reverence and rhetoric generally reserved for the life of the Buddha," it began. No publisher has so far seen fit to stick this on the back cover, but I've always liked those opening lines. Quite appropriate too since I certainly did idolize Janis, saw her life as exemplary, and wrote about it as such. Exemplary of *what* is the subject of this book.

A more indulgent eye might perhaps be cast on this portrait of Janis if I were to say that *Piece of My Heart* is, *mutatis mutandis,* a collection of scenes from the life of a sanctified sinner. The life of a saint, in short. And if a humorless, self-trumpeting court quisling in a sisal rug like Amenhotep, Son-of-Hapu (an accountant, no less!) can be called a saint (and he has been) I don't see why this should seem such an extravagant claim. (Saint: a person recognized as being entitled to veneration or capable of interceding for men on earth.)

And, if Janis—instead of dying of an overdose in a seedy motel off Sunset Strip—had been a thirteenth-century abbess, martyred in an exotic fashion by Visigoths, then *Piece of My Heart* is just the sort of book that (had I been Eusebius or St. Jerome) might have served as the first step towards her canonization.

Admittedly, Janis's was not the life of a saint as the Papal See decrees these matters. An anchorite of debauchery and licentiousness, her relentless pursuit of a good time often seemed an affliction as stringent as Catherine's fiery wheel. But to me she will always be larger than life, like the early Flemish painting where donors and local divines loom as enormous as the cathedrals or town walls next to which they stand. Janis's voice came upon her in that abandoned lighthouse turret like Gabriel at the Annunciation. And there I see her, like a Brobdingnagian Rapunzel, head leaning out of a medieval crenelated tower, crying: "Hey, man, I can sing!" Her death was a martyrdom for beliefs so preposterous they make the idea of sacrificing yourself in the name of established religion seem almost opportunistic.

Now a saint's life should perhaps be written in Latin, but, failing this, I sought a sacralingua suited to my consecrated purpose, and believed I had found one in the celestial mythologies of Mircea Eliade, full of Iglulik shamans fondling their own skeletons and shapeshifting animistic voices. To this kozmic brew I added a quantity of the old Keltic knotwork which wound about and about in a New Grange whorl until soon enough it entwined itself around such diverse topics as taxonomic descriptions of the mental geography of airports, reflections on American civilization and its discontents, the more arcane Thoughts and Hallucinations of the Ages (Rabelais, Pirandello, Kierkegaard, Coleridge, et al.), and my own anguish at Janis's death.

Although the book was by now as massively overfreighted as a pharaoh's tomb ship, I remember thinking it still not quite luxuriant enough for my evangelical purposes. Some final touch was lacking. I soon found the solution in two books I'd nicked from a friend's collection — one about a beach in winter and the other a life of Antonin Artaud. I simply "sampled" phrases I was convinced were uncanny, and randomly sprinkled them onto the pages. The nacreous imbrication of helical conches and the peyote delirium of sacred Tarahumari runners (as perceived by a French madman on opium) . . . all this seemed, at the time, to be mysteriously preordained as part of the book.

However auspicious and sacramental these devices, they led to a somewhat hermetic and overwrought text, or so I thought. And thus, gentle reader, as we enter the catacomb with only the flickering light of a torch, I might offer to guide you through the labyrinth by illuminating certain passages. These fall into two categories: Words of the Kozmic One and Scenes from the Life.

The One Night Stand Existencialista with which the book opens was written as an introduction to the second edition.

The book proper begins with *Southern Tales* and *The Mechanics of Ecstasy*, which cover a tour of the South with Janis in 1970.

The third section, *The Caterpillar On the Leaf*, consists mainly of acid flashbacks to Haight-Ashbury.

Finally, *The Million Dollar Bash* recounts a tour by train across Canada in the Summer of 1970. Among the performers: the Grateful Dead, The Band, Delaney and Bonnie, Tom Rush, Buddy Guy and Eric Andersen. "The Blushful Hippocrene" was written by Jonathan Cott (with whom I wrote an account of the trip for *Rolling Stone*). The book ends with "Symbolic Wounds," a raunchy dialogue between Janis and Bonnie Bramlett about women in rock, men in general, horn players, cowboy boots, and silk sheets.

David Dalton
Delhi, N.Y.
May 1991

THE ONE NIGHT STAND

EXISTENCIALISTA

*. . . . and she had not forgotten that, if you drink from a bottle marked "poison,"
it is almost certain to disagree with you, sooner or later. However this bottle was
not marked "poison" . . . .*

Lewis Carroll, *Alice's Adventures in Wonderland*

the red squire lounge blues

e're in a bar somewhere in, uh . . . Tennessee, Missouri, Kansas, Calgary, Saskatoon . . . . It doesn't really matter. Right now I'm more interested in my motor-inn-cocktail-lounge list, you know, those imaginative names they dream up for the bar in your local Ramada Inn: "The Luau Lounge," "The Sir Sirloin Bar & Grill," "The Prairie Schooner," "The Tartan Room," "The Falstaff Pub," "Smuggler's Reef," "The Ready Room."

The tape is rolling. It usually is these days. A good thing, too, because I'm in no condition just now to recall much of anything, much less take notes. You never can tell what's going to happen next, can you? And really, when you think about it, everything is *interesting*.

Hey, dig the Astros singing "Dock of the Bay," man! How'n hell they ever get those, uh . . . (flowers?) *into* that wall? Carved red fuckin' wallpaper, man! And a suit of aluminum armor with the Alcoa coat of arms. Don't tell me this ain't the weirdest country on earth, man. The Rainy Taxi ain't got nothin' on us!

Even the philosophical discussion now under way in the Red Squire Lounge between Janis, two salesmen from Atlanta, an aspiring local black entertainer, and a stewardess from San Jose *uncannily* bears out axiom 6.5 from Wittgenstein's *Tractatus:* "All propositions are of the same value."

A *bit* hungover, admittedly. Janis recommends a bullshot. For starters, anyhow. A couple of aspirins. Maybe a Percodan. Yes, I definitely need something to attack the higher centers of pain. I have quite an extensive medicine chest at this point. I mean, we're on the bloody road, aren't we, and you know how hard it can be, especially for those of us who aren't performers. Just the grind of another place that you can't call home. By now I have come to believe that it *is* "all the same fuckin' day"—this from the sayings of the one-night-stand *existentialista* herself.

I'm up to half a bottle of Southern Comfort, Heaven Hill, whatever, a day. Janis has stopped sharing "her" bottle with me. Miss Generosity suggests, in her characteristically understated manner, that I get my own fuckin' bottle.

How I came to this pass began what seems like a lifetime ago, maybe *another* lifetime ago. . . .

A muggy New York morning in June 1970. I go down to meet Janis at the Chelsea Hotel. It is only 8:00 a.m., but Janis (her fluorescent feathers practically blinding at this time of day) is already downstairs, striding up and down the lobby in a state of alert amnesia. The lobby overflows with the bizarre art works with which past patrons have paid their bills. The desk clerk, who looks like he was written by William Burroughs, is listening impassively to five conversations at once. Janis insists that he "try that motherfucker's room again and tell him to get his ass down here or I'm gonna personally go up there and . . . and. . . . "

But before Janis can think of a fate horrible enough for we-don't-know-whom, she catches my eye. "Hey, man, you made it!" she says in her squeaky little girl tone of voice. Her in-person voice is just as suggestive as her singing voice, and her utter astonishment at my presence has the inflection—all at once—of two guerillas who've just made it through the lines in *For Whom the Bell Tolls*, a lovers' tryst after a quarrel, and the Haight Street lilt of "Hey, you're gettin' your shit together, too, *man*!"

"This is an item for 'Random Notes,' man—'Janis Joplin out of bed before John Cooke.' Course I *do* have a slight edge, seeing as *I* didn't get to bed, couldn't find anyone, *sob*, to go to bed *with*, in the whole of New-fuckin'-York, man. And I was lookin' *real* hard. What I wanna know is where are all those star fuckers I keep reading about in *Rolling Stone?* Aw, nobody wants an old chick like me, anyway. Come on, let's go get a drink. If we're going to get maudlin this early in the day, might as well do it drunk, right?"

It's one of those dark, dingy bars. The only other patrons look like they came in around the time the Dodgers moved to L.A., and have been there ever since. They are eyeing Janis, who seems totally unfazed by this barroom behavior and the startled amusement her appearance invariably provokes. As the two old boys down at the other end trade wisecracks at her expense, Janis makes herself *outrageously* at home. She commandeers the place instantly, making it so completely hers that it is the regulars who are begining to look out of place.

"Don't mind them, man, they're fans of mine," she cackles and orders the first round.

"Two double Jack Daniels for him, and two double Jack Daniels for me. No point in wasting time."

The four chunky glasses filled to the brim with amber potion look awesome. Janis crinkles her eyes, leans over them with a manic grin and smacks her lips, her tongue moving slowly across her wide mouth in a slow motion Zap animation that's positively lascivious.

"Now *that's* more like it! Well, David, welcome aboard the Pinball Blues Medicine Show! Roll up, ladies and gentlemen and see the impossible, death-defying feat as Janis Joplin glues herself together for the third round . . . only to get shot down again! Only kidding . . . I *think*. Hey, man. I hope you jerkoffs at *Rolling Stone* are not going to *demolish* me again like you did the last two times. That really *crushed* me, man, my own fuckin' people, *man! Twice* you fuckers did it to me."

Throwing myself on the mercy of the court, I go into my how-long-we-know-each-other-what-about-last-year-in-London-didn't-I-write-a-great-piece-about-the-Albert-Hall-concert rap.

"That was *probably* because I was fucking your roommate," she graciously retorts. She's still on a bat about *Rolling Stone*. The magazine seems to have taken on the significance of the military-industrial complex for Janis. I try, as best I can, to explain the fine distinctions between me and *Rolling Stone*. After a few suggestions—expletive deleted!—about what Jann Wenner can do with himself, Janis's tirade winds down to the inevitable apologies. Just had to get it off her chest, nothing personal, just a bit touchy these days, can you dig it, man?

Janis knocks back the first shot in one slug and hoists the second Jack Daniels, poised for the next toast. I'm still sipping my first, and Janis is eyeing me with suspicion. The bourbon tastes bitter, sickly sweet, like some poisonous liquid candy. And I haven't had breakfast. I'm wondering how I'm going to get the next sip down, never mind two glasses of this stuff.

"You planning on having a long relationship with that glass or are you going to drink it? Drink up, man. Maybe we can get another round in before John Cooke [*the band's road manager*] shows up and takes our bottle away."

"Uh . . . Janis, I can *not* drink two doubles of this stuff at eight in the morning. I mean, this is not my thing."

Janis suddenly becomes incredibly belligerent, as if I've personally insulted her.

"Don't gimme any of that hippie bullshit, man. Listen, motherfucker, you drink it or you're not coming on this tour. I've already got four hippies in this band sitting around their motel rooms smoking grass and listening to tapes and communing with the wallpaper. This is gonna be a *party*, man. Clark [*Pierson*] is the only cat in this band who ever wants to go *out*. I can't stand it, man! I'm a lonely old beatnik chick on the road and I want some *company*, man. I can't do this alone. Eighty-year-old bartenders givin' me dirty looks every time I walk in some sleazebag bar somewhere. Gettin' hit on by crackers right and left. And women, man, in the South hate me *on sight*."

I'm beginning to feel real bad about not finishing that first drink.

"Knock it back, man," Janis says sympathetically. "You can't *sip* this stuff at eight in the morning. That's Happy Hour shit."

By the time the limos arrive to take us to the airport I am definitely feeling no pain. I climb in with Janis, John Till [lead] and Brad Campbell [bass]. Both are wired to head sets and greet me—from their dimension—with hippie comraderie. John hands me his headset. Area Code 615, the crack Nashville session band are playing in The Synapse Lounge this morning, and hey, good buddy, these ol' boys are really *cookin'*. As we turn onto the Long Island Expressway, Brad slips his stereofoams on my head. It's Tranc, man, live from the Planet Debbie, beaming down—I swear—"Chim Chim Cheree!"

Janis is rolling her eyes, "Oh, *man*, you guys are not gonna do this all the way to Louisville, are you? Isn't anybody gonna *talk*, man, or am I gonna get left in *abject boredom* while you guys zone off into Transistor City?"

No one is paying any attention to "poor Janis." Another tape. We're on the Sowside, Chicago, now, and Amos Milbourn and the Chicken Shackers are really smokin' T 'n' T and drinkin' dynamite, tonight, fellahs, can you dig it? Yeah, of course Brad and John can dig it. It's just that ol' Boystown Blues Club tearing down the highway, chile, on the way to the next gig. Janis is decidedly not amused.

"Honey, you *promised* me you weren't gonna do this shit on this trip," Janis says so soulfully I take the headset off.

"Just trying to get to know the band, Janis," I say, apologizing about I'm not quite sure what.

"Well you don't have to try *that hard*, man. These cats are real basic. Shit, man, you rock writers are all alike. A bunch of frustrated ghee-tar players. But *dig it*, that's *their* gig, man. Yours, *I am assuming*, is to write an article for *Rolling Stone*. Besize, honey, this is *Janis's* tour so . . . you better pay attention to me, *motherfucker!*"

She chuckles and starts singing, " 'I want a little piece for Janis, behbeh, can't I get a *little* somethin' for Janis, right now?' Don't mind me, man, I'm just fuckin' with ya . . . Now where'n the hell did I put that lighter . . . ? Probably left it in that bar. I'm *real* sloppy. Lose more damn things in bars. Left a wallet with a grand in it in a bar last week. Just can't seem to hang onto *anything*, man."

In desperation Janis dumps her bag onto the floor of the limo. Its contents are truly awesome. Janis has a bag lady's compulsion to carry her whole life with her. There are two movie stubs, a pack of cigarettes, an antique cigarette holder, several motel and hotel room keys, a box of Kleenex, a compact and various make up cases (in addition to a bunch of eyebrow pencils held together with a rubber band), an address book, dozens of bits of paper, business cards, match box covers with phone numbers written in near-legible barroom scrawls, guitar picks, a bottle of Southern Comfort (empty), a hip flask, an opened package of complementary macadamia nuts from American Airlines, cassettes of Johnny Cash and Otis Redding, gum, sunglasses, credit cards, aspirin, assorted pens and writing pad, a corkscrew, an alarm clock, a copy of *Time*, and two hefty books—Nancy Milford's biography of Zelda Fitzgerald and Thomas Wolfe's *Look Homeward, Angel*.

While Janis continues to root through her bag, I pick up *Look Homeward, Angel*, and read the blurb on the back: "A novel depicting the coming of age of Eugene Gant—his boyhood in North Carolina and his growing passion to experience life." It occurs to me that Janis's touchiness about her "serious reading habits" has more to do with her interest in these books as exemplary lives, American saints' lives, than the usual rock posture of anti-intellectualism.

I am still quite spaced from my liquid breakfast, and although it has numbed considerably the awkward business of injecting oneself into a new group the first day out, the buzz is unexpectedly like an acid flash. Everything seems impossibly remote and microscopically close at the same time. Colors are blurry at the edges, but with a slight iridescent *halo*. And keep your eye on the red Volkswagen! The decaying structures of the World's Fair to the left of us look very *meaningful* and poignant, like a ruin from the future.

Flipping through *Look Homeward, Angel*, the epigraph reaches out to me with its fine italic hand. It suddenly seems loaded with associations. The significance of life is here. Definitely!

> . . . . *Remembering speechlessly we seek the great forgotten language,*
> *the lost lane-end into heaven, a stone, a leaf, an unfound door.*
> *Where? When?*
> *O lost, and by the wind grieved, ghost, come back again.*

Flight 729 to Louisville. As engrossed as she is in her book, the arrival of the trolley bearing our mid-morning *refreshments* catches Janis's attention. She eyes the shrunken bottles of Johnny Walker and Jim Beam that are now arrayed before us in military formation with the unhealthy interest of, say, a Congo headhunter at the arrival of a new batch of missionaries.

"We'll take a case of those," Janis says, pointing to the Lilliputian bottles of Southern Comfort on the tray.

"I'm sorry, ma'am," says the stewardess with resigned deadpan. Janis accepts the bottles allotted to her and announces to no one in particular, "Shit, I practically *own* that company, man!"

At the Louisville airport Janis wants to buy some papers and souvenirs at the airport gift shop, but John Cooke proclaims with West Point authority: "Anybody not *outside* when the transportation arrives gets left behind."

"Oh, *moan*," says Janis (her own Crumb cartoon). Cooke is unmoved. "And that means *you*, Miss Joplin."

"Hey, we still got time to get us another bottle, man," Janis tells me in a conspiratorial stage whisper. We make a quick run to the liquor store and finally *clank* (Janis doesn't believe in packaging) into the station wagon that's taking us to the Holiday Inn in downtown Louisville.

I can barely make it up to my room, and it's *still* "the same fucking day."

Half an hour later, it's Janis on the house phone.

"Whatcha doin', honey?"

"Uh . . . passing out . . ."

Janis is horrified at this breach of alcoholic etiquette. "You can't *lie down*, man. You're gonna miss the whole show if you take a nap now. C'mon down, man, and have an eye-opener. There's a real swingin' crowd in the Derby Lounge," she cackles, "and they've got the Mets game on. I'm *sure* you wouldn't want to miss *that*."

She is sitting alone at the only occupied table in the place. A crowd of very Southern gentlemen are hanging out at the bar watching the game. They check out my hair and clothes (standard hippie issue) and I realize we're not in New York any longer.

"I have to make a confession to you; I did have an *ulterior* motive for draggin' you down here," says Janis as I sit down. "You know somethin', man? They wouldn't *let* me sit at the bar."

"Why would you want to sit with those guys, anyway, Janis?"

"Oh, you're just seein' Southern manhood in action, man. What I was talking about was comin' in here and gettin' treated *mean*. Got treated rude and mean the moment I walked into this place."

"I don't believe that, Janis, it's probably a, uh, hotel regulation or something."

"*Honey* . . . "

"Who would treat you mean? You're the star-in-residence."

"Honey, to them I'm just a chick who is hung over at 11:00 in the morning. My hair isn't combed, I'm wearin' funny lookin' clothes, plus I'm wearin' *feathers*. I walk in here and say I want a drink. These people don't want to *see* me, baby. I mean, let's *face it*, they don't want me in here—period. So there's three old cats sayin', 'What is this chick doin' here and *why*?' They'd just as soon be talkin' about the Mets game and they don't want this chick walkin' in with *bells* on and a big sack of beads.

"There's the snide remarks I'm not supposed to hear, but *loud* enough, of course, *for* me to hear. Everybody gets it, man. Gettin' treated like a hippie, that's what I'm talkin' about.

"They don't know I'm a Popstar. They don't even relate to Popstar*dom*."

I'm beginning to realize this is not going to be your standard *Rolling Stone* interview. Janis is *always* on. There's none of that "let's get this interview shit out of the way and then we can relax" business.

And she is saying the most *amazing* things! She is almost cinematic in her descriptions of people, places and situations; her stories, little dramatic interludes with Janis doing all the voices. I can't get all this down *and* participate, and Janis demands participation. She now considers me her drinking buddy, "the cat from *Rolling Stone* who's interviewing me," and the guy fire-breathing Southern bartenders aren't gonna mess with (Yikes!).

Excusing myself, I stumble off to locate my tape recorder. The only solution is going to be to record *everything*. It's the only decent (and feasible) and existentialist thing to do.

I slip the gun-metal black Sony on the table as casually as possible, but there's just no way of doing things unobtrusively around Janis. Her reaction to this *thing* among the drinks, nuts, magazines, packs of cigarettes and coasters could not be more astonished. She scans its alien presence with wary curiosity, as if it were a transistorized replica of the Kaaba emitting verses from the Koran.

"*Lord!*" she implores. "Don't tell me *you're* gettin' wired for sound, now, too!"

Janis's natural mode of conversation was quite a work of art. She'd launch into a long rap about the decline in swizzle stick design, complete with vivid descriptions of the ones with flamingos, the palm tree motif in Florida as opposed to the West Coast, etc. Then it's on to the smell of eucalyptus trees around her house in Larkspur, an Antonioni movie she saw last week, Carson McCullers, the reunion concert with Big Brother and Nick Gravenites at the Fillmore West last Spring, life on the road and *life as such*. She was also *very* sharp, a whizzer, as Danny Fields described her.

However much make-believe Janis wove into her myth, its very unreliability as fact was, in the end, less important than its success as fiction. The preposterous has in any case always been the gen-u-ine homespun American article, and Janis's delight in it was reflected in the ludicrous shifts in scale with which she narrated her pratfall past as a series of seductions by men, by women, by art, by music, by books, by drugs, by drink, by introspection, even by her own voice, and all strung out in geographical order like those souvenir maps illustrated with vignettes of lassoing cowboys, adobe villages and leaping salmon.

An almost Rabelaisian inventory of fabulistic caricatures surrounds Janis, buzzing with noisy denial. "Just can't be, now, no, no, no, it just can't be!" is not just Janis's protest, but that of anyone who hears, in the soundtrack turning endlessly in their head, the voice of what Kerouac called "that inscrutable *future* Americans are always longing and longing for."

janis, jimi and the square root of the blooz

> And the blues have bin goin' on for the centuries and centuries. The blues was written in years and centuries ago. And they will always last.
>
> **B.B. King**

Now, all you hep cats, this here's the story of how the blues came to earth. Long ago, in the inter-archival primeval rain forest, all peoples, talkin' animals 'n' Thunder Beings, they all be livin' together in harmony. Folks back then was always happy, laughin',

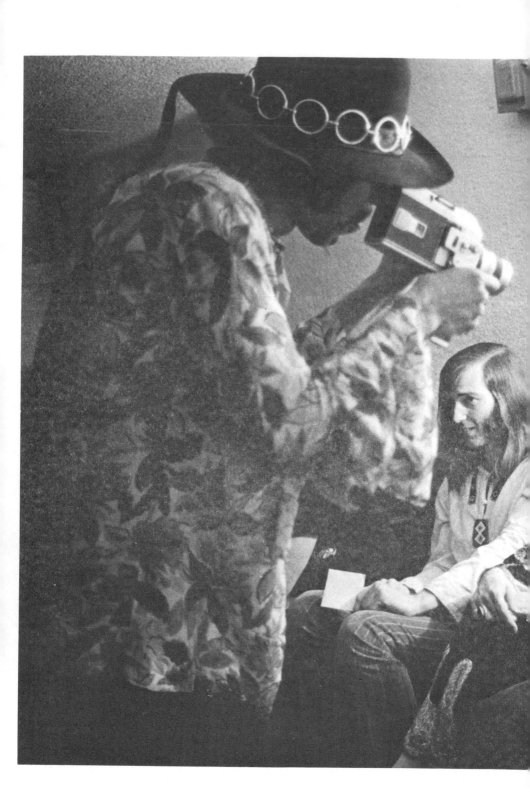

Backstage, Winterland, 1967 with Sam Andrew and Fug, KenWeaver.
Jimi Hendrix makes home movie [JIM MARSHALL]

playin' and jivin' with themselves. They never quarreled, stole, lied or cheated and Ol' Man Trouble, he never came roun' their door.

Now, one day the tribe, see, decide to have themselves a party and the elders at this festivity decide to entertain the villagers. Each dude would do his thing to entertain the peoples. Now this here's where all the troubles we have in the world have started.

The witch doctor, bein' fanned by fourteen nu-bile priestesses—he be gettin' mighty high on primo Malawi weed 'n' Mango brandy, y'unnerstan'?—he out there, jus' shakin' his rattle, which is made of shells, feathers, colored seeds 'n' greasy chicken bones, 'n' he intonin' a prayer in a unknown jive language that bin lost.

So, after he bite the head off a alligator, the show begin. Up come Lizard Son and the Kozmic Konkubine ladies, 'n' he do a few cool polyrhythm type riffs on a drum he made from the Divine Serpent's ear with the womens doin' four part harmonies, like.

"That be nothin'," say Cousin Zac, 'n' he do his fantabulistic brake dance.

"Looky here," say Baron Sunday—who got on his boneyard threads—'n' he be with his hippie bride, Rainbow, 'n' they make such a leap into the atmospheah that they don' come down for 'roun' two weeks.

"Okeh, fellahs, you all ready for the Angeltown Soun'?"

Then Sony Walkman tell the peoples the outtasight story of the Talkin' Skull accompanyin' hisself with all kinda shape changin', 'n' when he come to the punch line, "I tol' yous you best keep yo mouth shut!" at which they all fall on the groun' laughin' 'n' laughin'.

Now everyone be thinkin', "Who gonna top that?"

Up jump Papa Bo Jingle Jangle and he say, "You ain't seen diddly shit. What I have here, ladies 'n' gentlemens, this gonna really blow yo minds."

"Yes?" they say, anticipatin' what he about to put up. "What you got in that swamp bag, chile?"

"De blooze!"

"The wha?"

He don' say nothin', but an evil grin did come over his face 'n' he pull out his ax 'n' begin to wail.

32

"Woke up this smornin' . . . ."
And there never bin peace in the barnyard since.

We're talking about the deep blues, them real primordial, pre-lapsarian blues, the ones that began when the seventh son (the original Delta bluesman) began moaning and twanging, presumably while God was resting, on the seventh hour of the seventh day. Or, at the very least, the blues contemporary with the expulsion of Adam and Eve along with their harp-blowing serpent from the Garden of Eden.

The blues have been traced all the way back to Ibo war chants, the lament of the first transported slave, the legendary Bo Weevil plantation, and the coming of the P&O line to Mississippi. This obsession with roots is not just the archival fixation of scholars. It is a source of inspiration to every blues singer. The quest for the mother lode of the blues is central to all blues mythology, and to its powers of regeneration.

Although no less apocryphal than Ye Olde Englishe auto-harp Appalachia of Joan Baez or the Stones equally imaginary Rock Kingdom of the U.S.A., this belief in the existence of an ancient well of the blues has meant that, by returning to the *source*, each generation has been able to re-imagine and hence re-invent it.

Now, the so-called Second Coming of the Blues in the sixties was only one more imagined recreation of its primal cry. It followed gospel, jazz, be-bop and post-war R&B, and preceded much of rock, soul, disco, punk and neo-rockabilly. While the British Invasion and soul found their brand new beat in revamped versions of rock and gospel, Janis Joplin and Jimi Hendrix chose to encode their message in a form at once more intimate and more traditional—the ancient sorrows of the blues. The rigid 12-bar formula, 4/4 time and repeated three line verses provided a solid framework within which they unleashed the most emotionally explicit and expressive form rock had ever taken.

They used their high tension, brain scan blues as a telegraphic code. Transmitting themselves through their own nervous systems, they abandoned themselves to the fevers of electricity. In an extreme and terminal development of the art of the blues, Janis and Jimi represent that fragile beyond-which-there-is-nothing when feeling and technique are in perfect accord, just as Bessie Smith and Robert Johnson were consummations of that exquisite moment in the blues as a developing art form.

In transmitting the catechisms of the blues, Janis and Jimi were recapitulating and revamping all that had gone before. But confessin' the blues the way they did had little in common with the faithful replications of blues purists. British rock antiquarians were the principle disseminators of this "pure," retro-archival blues, a symptom of that particularly English fascination with mouldy and obsolete forms of American music. Like folk music, the primary impulse of these excavations was to recreate a lost, ideal culture uncontaminated by the present.

A *nostalgie de la Delta* (roughly equivalent to the sentimental attachment of city dwellers to vine-covered cottages) has inevitably clung to white blues.

As the music of the itinerant and the displaced, the blues is predicated on change, and with the drifter's mistrust of permanence, its moveable parts are *designed* for possible alterations in one's circumstances. The generic form of the blues is very forgiving; change is the constant, and implanted in its formal 12-bar parenthesis are receptor sites allowing for endless deformations of structure. From jazz, its cerebral offspring, to its bastard child, rock 'n' roll, its protean adaptions demonstrate that the blues actually *gains* by translation.

Set in the past (a past in which things, money, lovers and youth have been lost) to disarm the pain and phrased with self-mocking bravado, the blues has always tried to distance itself from its troubles. It takes the long way round.

Backstage Winterland with Noel Redding of the Jimi Hendrix Experience [JIM MARSHALL]

Caught in the limbo of repeated wrongs, the obligatory repetition of the first line of each verse is both sentence and release, fate and freedom, curse and exorcism. It is this deadpan formality that makes the blues a lyrically consoling form, an anachronism. To turn the blues from its plaintive, formal reassurance is to expose its knotty gnarled roots; to digress, distress and strain to exhaustion the hieroglyphics of emotional language.

You never hear in Janis the sort of ersatz bloozspeak affected by many white singers. Janis never "de train come in de station" like Mick does, but then for the Stones quotation marks are their way of being *sincere*, just as the absence of irony is for Janis a sign of possession, immersion, naivete and willful abandon. England, in any case, has simply never been able to produce the same kind of direct current.

Janis detonated the hysteria latent in the blues. For this "betrayal" of the blues code of cool she was criticized more

On stage with Tina Turner at the Rolling Stones
Madison Square Garden concert, 1969 [AMALIE ROTHSCHILD]

by whites than blacks. "Janis Joplin sings the blues as hard as any black person," said B.B. King. "It's about the war between the sexes."

Unrestrained by formal or cultural pressures, Janis and Jimi attempted to alchemize out of the elementary table of the blues its crystal core. They invoked the eerie *feel* of the interacting layers of the blues—the blues spirits. But through this collapse in space and time, unstable elemental forces materialized that summoned up the spectral ferocity of the lost West African Deep Blues. It was a blues hallucinated to convey the intensity with which Janis and Jimi had heard its compelling voice for the first time.

"They were playing that fifties crap on the radio," Janis said. "It seemed so shallow, all oop-boop. It had nothing. Then I heard Leadbelly and it was like a flash. It *mattered* to me."

It was as if they wanted to experience not just the blues but the original impulse that created it: the violence, eroticism, craziness and sputtering of rage before the blues had been codified and ironized. An increasing tendency to irrationality, a shattering of the blues form, the iridescent shimmer of particles left in its wake . . . . Janis and Jimi attempted to make the blues conform to the chaos around them. But they found in the blues a succession of restraints similar to those of the society that both confined and excluded them, and as embedded in the form as the notes sentenced to its 12 bars. It's the same old fatal destination, the concubinage of the blues.

Trains cars, buses, crossroads, loss, distance and loneliness. The panoramic language of the blues. The song of the ramblin' man, his direction always away—from his home, his baby, his roots.

It's the drifters escape; a myth of freedom and a disdain for boundaries with which Janis profoundly identified.

The wandering *griot* storyteller at the bottom of blues mythology knows that the further you travel down that road the more the loss of what you've left behind will prey on you. He sings his song to console, vindicate and absolve himself. That his story is "confessed" to others does not relieve him of his isolation or disguise his own awareness that the true audience is the self one tries to evade.

The repetition of injustices included in the blues form seems to say that by simply depicting the way things *are* and passing on this self-mocking message, things *might* change. And the blues is about going through changes—changes of heart, changes of mind, changing times. At its core is the idea of changing places, seeing another point of view, and as the Kozmic Blues of the rock apocalypse, Janis's blues were about the urgency of transforming yourself. Her message to herself and to us was: *you must change!*

The singer gives voice to the unnamable and prepares you for *it* when the time comes. As Albert King says, "The blues tell a true story. They sing about the real mean and rotten things that can happen to you. If you don't know about 'em now, you're *gonna* know about 'em. Some of these kids have never had the blues and they're asking you to tell them what it's like. Perhaps blues expresses what they can't say."

The blues are an animal language. Howlin' Wolf wailin' and moanin' the blues; a croak, a cry, a sigh. Guitars whine, talk and wail, harps moan, honk and whistle like the engineer's quill. Voices veer off into noises.

It's blues the hue of sky meeting horizon and no end in sight. It's the bluh of the blues and the ooooohs! of the blues not to mention the *I'm losin' you* of the blues. It's a disease of the self by its lonesome:

> *You makes your bed hard, baby, and calls it ease*
> *The blues is just a funny feeling*
> *Yet some folks call it a mighty bad disease.*
>
> **Lightnin' Hopkins**

Big Brother's rehearsal loft, San Francisco, 1967. Left to right: Sam Andrew, Peter Albin, Janis, Dave Getz, Jim Gurley [JIM MARSHALL]

Like a powerful solvent, trouble *melts* the words before your eyes. Everything, through its liquid gaze, dissolves into tears:

> *I'm a pterodactyl*
> *I'm an abominable snowman*
> *Cryin' for your love . . . .*
>
> **Peter Albin,** "Caterpillar"

Like Elijah's mantle, the hand-me-down adaptability of the blues is the riteful inheritance of all shape shifters, for only those who have first transformed themselves have the right to bend "reality" to their will. The suppression of the natural and the invocation of the shadowy overtones of the supernatural is the magic, hoodoo habit of the blues with regard to spirit.

The blues is a mystic language of spells, curses, hexes of the old West African religion: ju jus, macumbas, gris gris, Black Cat Bone, goofer dust, Little John the Conquerer root. Those engrained superstitions, saturated in mojo magic and distilled into spirit, are thinly hidden beneath its funky complaints about women, men, whiskey, money and the mean ol' world that its earthy cynicism mocks.

Janis and Jimi revealed what the blues (for reasons of caution, irony, superstition) deliberately concealed. For some, they did so too explicitly, betraying the unwritten "but-I-was-cool" law of blues self-preservation—not to mention the more ominous personal dangers involved in this transgression.

Of course, looking into the void and Bardo-gazing were an indulgent pastime of the First Great Psychedelic Age and the speed freak prairie fires of the late sixties, but Janis and Jimi wanted to *actually set foot* in this Existential hole-in-being, a fascination that was backed by their own confidence that negativity would pull them through. These lethal risks were, of course, only too well known to the blues. "If it weren't for bad luck, I wouldn't have no luck at all" is, after all, its central joke.

And it is just this zero that's at the heart of everything around which the blues tiptoes. At its center is a maelstrom that Janis and Jimi parodied in their lives, but from which they did not emerge. It is the snaky bloozspeak that treads with such desperate agility around the things it howls about. But in Janis and Jimi it reached a state of frenzy, and moved them towards the implicit tragedy that the blues have always invoked, but carefully deflected.

This darkening of the atmosphere and intensification of passion is the ancient stony face of the blues contorted by a lethal feedback. A sort of electric shock treatment to make the old bones of the blues get up and walk again, and to raise up Lazarus, just one more time.

janis in boystown

The raucous, bottle totin', pool shootin', "hiya boys!" good time girl that Janis projected was a flagrant inversion of the androgynous postures affected by rock 'n' roll's male guitar stars and lead singers. The early Elvis gave off ambiguous sexual signals.(So did his idol, James Dean.) From Elvis's (I just wanna be your) teddy bear huggableness to Bowie's extraterrestrial transvestism, rock 'n' roll had always considered male androgyny to be axiomatic.

The male aesthetic saw androgyny as a sign of sensuality and social defiance that released the tensions imposed by conventional sexual taboos. It also served to bond male stars to an audience that had always been, for the most part, young girls. But performers like Little Richard, Mick Jagger and David Bowie, by incorporating effeminate mannerisms into their acts, also tended to assimilate the role women might have played in rock.

When Janis arrived in Boystown with her tough babe, one-of-the-guys, biker mama swagger, she got a very cool reception from the Bop Street gang. By gad, sir, there's a *girl* in the club house and she's behaving just like one of *us!* Girls were just not, how shall we put it, *equipped* for this kind of thing.

The mates weren't exactly prepared for this role reversal business—or the circular reasoning involved. There was a place for women in the "music biz," all right—as torch *chanteuses*, teen angels, back up singers, Mary Quant dollies, song stylists, auto harp/dulcimer strumming folk madonnas, "girl groups," and even "singer-songwriters" like Joni and Carole.

Rock Inc.'s experience of women extended for the most part to waitresses, stewies, fans, flacks, groupies, or, that comic condition, rock wives. No one, to tell the truth, was ready for this full-blooded, hell-on-wheels comraderie. "Are you a boy or are you a girl?" took on an entirely new meaning in Janis's case. She was too "butch," they said. This was Mickey Spillane in drag, for chrissakes!

Janis's brazen hussy debauchee was simply not as acceptable as the effeminacy affected by rock 'n' roll's male stars. Female stars were assumed, by the very nature of the passive roles they played, to be sexually "selfsufficient"—fulfilled *by the desire they generated in others*. Women did not need to include in their sexual projections any additional cultural codes.

The roles imposed on women were in many ways more restricting than the "I'm all right Jack" codes of male behavior, yet women were permitted to be assertive only if they couched their rebellion in self-parody. Even Mae West's anomalous, boa-butch posturing was allowed to flourish solely in the context of the camp put-on of female impersonation. Janis's solution was characteristically extreme: she was going to *become* one of the guys.

Unlike male singers who at least *appeared* to create their own images, the styles and even the personas of women singers were assumed to have been molded by men. According

From Monterey Pop. *June 1967 with Peter Albin* [P.A. PENNEBAKER ASSOCIATES]

to the Phil Spector Wall of Boys Effect, it was taken for granted that women were incapable of functioning without male know-how. In this Spectoral mythology women were a sort of beautiful void on which the maestro as manager, producer, arranger or songwriter could project his fantasies at will. Assumed to be vulnerable, defenseless and hopelessly unfulfilled, women were *defined by their deficiencies*. And made to admit as much in song.

Behind all this was the inference that "chick singers" were interchangeable. Women in pop music were an amorphous, sexual substance that, by definition, needed molding by men. In a sort of Vinylized Virgin Mary complex, Phil's seminal Brill-iance impregnated the girl groups with his "boy genius-ness."

But Janis invented herself, and in so doing she created something so exquisitely manifest that it transcended the patronizing context of managers and producers, songwriters, bands, arrangers and publicists. Her very existence seemed to dismiss them by default.

Janis made every one of the songs she sang *hers* by the sovereign right of her charisma. Even when they had already been hits for someone else, she appropriated them as her own story: "Ball And Chain," "Maybe," "Little Girl Blue," and "Piece Of My Heart." Janis extended the reflections of female sensibility implicit in her songs, and achieved a consummation of the material so definitive that few singers have even *attempted* them since.

Her exaggerations turned the love song into a lament for civilization and repression (its offspring). If Janis seemed to be chronically seeking answers from someone incapable of responding ("Blindman, show me the way to go home"), this very exhibition of helplessness became in itself a value and transformed the desperate abandonment of Janis's singing into a moral issue: "Mothers, tell your children, don't you do what I have done" . . . . She made the resourcelessness of

With Grace Slick, San Francisco, 1967 [JIM MARSHALL]

women political.

The fissioned notes and loaded pauses, the slippage as her voice skids over a note that, out of frustration, abandons language altogether, these ventriloqual shifts in Janis's vocal identity reflected the unnerving despair of someone thwarted by biological destiny, and constantly taunted by the possibility, even the assumption, of failure.

Her ability to sing more than one note at a time (by splitting it into two or three inflections) and her hesitation blues pitch created a mood of latency and anticipation that Janis took to the limit in "Ball And Chain." It was a sonic suspense that fused the mental vertigo of sexual passion and the psychic suspension of drugged states into an oceanic sensation of euphoria. Emotional states became inseparable.

A sort of female impersonator (the Judy Garland effect), Janis acted herself out as the sexy, erotic and glamorous star she thought she was meant to be (and that audiences came

With Michael J. Pollard [JOHN FISHER]

to demand of her). She wore her bracelets, necklaces, and gold sling-back heels like a string of adjectives. Who could write a single line about Janis without using one of those epithets she dangled so seductively before us, a nervous predicate sheathed in descriptions (hooker pumps, neon feathers), and decked out in a large hyperbole (along with several of the gaudiest dangling modifiers she could find). Janis's ironic, ambivalent idea of glamour often bordered on kitsch. It was a combination of folklore and trash, the high-heeled babe with a heart of gold.

Janis was not the first of these gen-u-wine A-meri-kin Medicine Shows. She was in a long tradition of snake oil fake sincerity, tableauxed history and the Wild West nostalgia of Buffalo Bill, Mark Twain and Teddy Roosevelt. The sexuality implicit in her ultimate incarnation as Pearl (the " used" look) was a commentary on her role as a female star, just as her early Big Brother "sackcloth and ashes" get-ups, accessorized with a necklace made of chicken bones, had identified her with hippies, beats, blacks, indians—the fellaheen of the world.

Janis eventually abandoned her hippie threads. Hippie was too exclusive, too elitist; it was cultish and dowdy. She came to want something more mythic—a broader, more inclusive, more American image. Hippie, by definition, was just not universal enough. Janis's rejection of the hippie aesthetic in favor of a more conventional, self-deprecatingly tawdry personal style had more to do with her ambivalent embracing of stardom than any coherent idea of fashion. Pearl, the character Janis conjured up in the last year of her life, was the culmination of a honky-tonk image she had been working on since her first taste of true stardom at the Monterey Pop Festival. Janis shed the hippie/beatnik clothes worn at Saturday afternoon's performance for Sunday night's gold lamé dress, and it was this shift—from hippie threads to hooker flash—that marked the arrival of Pearl.

Janis did not want to be a cult hero.

With David Niehaus during Carnival in Rio de Janeiro
February 1970 [PAULO NEVES/COURTESY OF RICHARD HUNDGEN]

ball and chain

Janis insisted on following the bright, colorblind, toenail party of love. Like the fantasy worlds of Gothic Romances and Coke commercials, her notion of love was of such excessive proportions, so extreme and absurd, that it transcended not just the real world but also any real possibility of satisfaction. Somehow her arias of unrequited love and tableaux of eternal bliss just couldn't survive the shell-thin air outside her songs.

Janis *believed* every one of those dime store romances. Gimme that love! That was really the whole story. Corny, I guess, but Janis was just about the corniest person I ever met. She had attained fortune cookie Confucianism.

Every time, it was the same thing: "Oh, honey, I'm in love with this great big bear of a man, *uhn!* Met him in San Jose. Can you believe it, he was cleaning the pool at the Ramada Inn!" Naturally, when you met the guy he'd turn out to be some junkie-type from Laguna Beach, and after a while you wondered why she involved herself with these complete assholes. Maybe she'd gotten used to being unhappy; maybe if she found someone who actually cared about her she'd get bored out of her skull. "Too much ain't enough!" as they say in Texas.

No one, in any case, was *enough*. Nothing would ever be enough for Janis. And as far as being disappointed goes, every time was like the first time: "You'll never believe what that motherfucker *did* to me! To *me*, man, after all I did for him. All I wanted, man, was . . . ."

Janis wanted to make up for the pain of a lifetime in one love affair; she was trying to get even with a town. Her life was the kind of Wild West soap opera that even Calamity Jane couldn't get away with. And Janis was *so* fragile. It just seemed like every time something went wrong, that big, ugly, sprawling oil town would loom up and say, "We know you, and we'll always be the truth about you." Port Arthur was gonna get the last laugh no matter what. A town, especially your hometown, always has the last laugh.

Even in the funky world of San Francisco, Janis had been a primitive, an islander growing up like Topsy. Unlike her fellow Texan, Chet Helms, Janis was never at home anywhere, a situation that seemed to get progressively worse as fame and success caught up with her. In London, Janis was a freak, a novelty act something like James Brown.

There was never a "here," for Janis because here, like home, was something yet to be. There was only *there*, and neither her childhood nor her future were getting any smaller, they were, if anything, enlarging themselves. Perhaps Pearl was meant to be that portable darkness; that calm, still point at the center of her immense contradictions.

Janis's past was her ghostly lover, and it always seemed like singing would deliver this phantom, fictional lover to her *tonight* and nothing would ever part them again. Port Arthur taught her that the beloved object (like the audience) is always at a distance. The only possible consummation is *towards* it, and *away* from where you are. I want it now! (but not here).

Sometimes it seemed as if Janis felt that human relationships were a sort of distraction. Pearl didn't need them; Janis's lush fantasy life generated only insubstantial reflections, robbing her life of real events and other people.

Janis mirrored her past, throwing all her pain and humiliation back at us in shattered images. It was as if she would only be complete when these relentless reflections were seen and absorbed by others, and thus ceased to be.

Real lovers were something that threatened to drag one back into the sordid details and banal resolutions of everyday life, and specimens of manhood as preposterous as those Janis invokes in her lyrics *could* only exist in songs. Her real life lovers, even the most intense of them, were disposable, as if the actuality of romance was somehow a debasement, a crude, mundane metaphor for her conception of what romance must be.

Janis chose not to simplify, resolve or reconcile her conflicts—something she was, in any case, constitutionally unable to do. She kept everything in the air, ambivalent and *alive*. The last thing she wanted to give up was this seductive presentation of unsatisfied desire.

"I think everything that happened to her was just too much in the end," Janis said of Zelda Fitzgerald. "What I'm trying to say is that she had all these romantic aspirations and stuff and they all *really* happened to her eventually. So that what I think is, that that just freaked her out, it's like having a dream about something and then it actually happens."

The energy and comic desperation of Janis's singing, with its petulant, mocking exclamation points, ultimately turned torch songs into an indictment of romantic love. She showed us true romance to the point of horror—the carnival shooting gallery's petrified targets of happiness—and obliged us to feel the tragedy of poor lovers who stake everything on a love as perishable and corruptible as its very object, the flesh.

Janis believed in the happily-ever-afterness of love. She created tableaux of love the way an Amsterdam prostitute, in the picture windows of the red light district, sets the stage with such emblematic objects as lamps, armchairs, a tv, vases of flowers. She saw her longings the same way that whorehouses see desire—as a series of fixed obsessions. Repetition, far from dulling these illusions, created only more accumulations of reverence (and debasement) for the imaginary object of desire.

Memory, in a sense, supplants reality, and it was in pursuit of its remote promise that Janis would spend her life. This

she did with whomever would let her—and in *any* number of unlikely places and conditions.

She saw the love lives of others through windows—the picture window of the splitlevel life or, more often, the windshield of a truck on its way to someplace else. It was as if feelings that touched too deeply could only be glimpsed: "Sittin' down by my window, lookin' out at the rain . . . ."

"Bobby McGee" is a widescreen kaleidoscopic movie shot from a moving vehicle. Janis rushes by, "from the Kentucky coal mines to the California sun," in a panorama of American lives and life styles, a chorus of mimicked inflections in a rock 'n' roll ballad remaking of "This Land Is Your Land." Even the collage of different voices and styles — Tammy Wynette twang to gospel, country, rock, folk—is her way of inhabiting these unlived lives in her imagination.

One can imagine Janis as one of those possessed, imprinted birds pumping her wings furiously, ceaselessly across Texas, New Mexico, Arizona, California, ignoring the seductions of the cowboys, oil riggers and semi drivers waving their hats to her from below, driven onwards, and, always, inexorably, *away*. The states reflected in her eyes as she pants, "Got to get there, got to get there, got to get there, gotta, gotta get there." She knows it is noon, yet the sun is just rising . . . so she heads West—to get that sun over head where it should be.

Janis's telescopic fantasies and sentimental *mise-en-scenes* were only slightly more foamy versions of childhood's cast of imaginary playmates. Her songs became phantom lovers of the equally imaginary Pearl, who could, almost literally, bend reality to her will.

We get the chilling sense that, for Janis, "take the stars out of the night" is not hyperbole, and this feeling beckons us out of ourselves and back into the great world of lost childhood, a place where we can make the world up all over again. It is the child's belief in the communion of all things and the continuum of pleasure.

Those who believe they have been denied a childhood nurture the child in themselves, and the stage became for Janis a gigantic play space on which she could act out her postponed childhood. For Janis, singing was believing. Her voice, with its emotional onomatopoeia, irresistibly pulled us into the wake of her song as she summoned up for us a world of future possibilities, freedom and sensuality.

There no longer existed that distance between singer and song that in blues stimulated reflection. But in decimating these limits, Janis also removed whatever barriers might have mediated her feelings, and consequently undermined the coherence of her own life.

Like the pact between lover and love (or audience and star) the conspiracy between Janis and Pearl was unshakeable. All

boundaries had been erased. As she fused herself to Pearl, their magnetic currents generated a solipsistic universe; the space between Janis and her myth collapsed. Mass success meant that the exhibition of her pain and loss was now also a performance, rendering ultimate meaning unfathomable. Behind the bravura of her immaculately conceived heroine, Janis looked small and frail and lonely — dwarfed by the audacity of her own creation.

"I'm selling my heart!" Janis told *Newsweek*. But it wasn't only her heart she was selling (hearts have long been a torch singer's commodity). It was *herself*, that supreme erotic artifact of rock. But Janis's inclusiveness ("I'm into me plus they're into me, and everything comes together.") had the reciprocal imperative that *everybody* must love Janis, and some days you wanted to say what must have been obvious even to Janis: that you can't love everybody and you can't want everybody to love you. Just like you can't love responsibility or formica.

Janis's unquestioning identification with the *self* she projected to her audience, and the uncanny synchronization of this self with her time, set in motion a spiral of confusion of identity that did not exclude her awareness of the consequences: "Maybe my audience can enjoy my music more if they think I'm destroying myself."

As her sense of persecution increased, Janis more and more took refuge in drugs. Threats no longer had to be *real* for Janis to react with irrational virulence. The couple laughing at the next table were laughing at Janis; a remark made by a roadie was taken as a personal insult. As her own life began to exhaust its meaning in public display, Janis was drawn into a state of acute self-awareness.

"Nobody would ever have fallen in love," wrote La Rochefoucauld," if they had not first read about it." Our notions of true love, derived, as they are from books, movies, magazines and songs, are, in the end, a form of parody. A recreation of an inversion of real love! Thus was Pearl the kozmic caricature of Janis.

> I read a story about some old opera singer once, and when a guy asked her to marry him, she took him backstage after she had sung a real triumph, with all the people calling for her, asked, "Do you think you could give me that?" That story hit me right, man. I know no guy ever made me feel as good as an audience. I'm really far into this now, really committed. Like, I don't think I'd go off the road for long now, for life with a guy no matter how good. Yeah, it's the truth. Scary thing to say though, isn't it?

Resigned to fulfilling her need for love by other means, a relationship came to mean something else for Janis. It was the unknown all, the *it*.

Like the old maid in Colette ("of the kind so in love with love that no love seems fine enough to them . . . they refuse themselves without deigning to explain their refusal"), Janis's self-denial became its own consecration. Her Book of Love conceived of *it* as an abstraction: something unattainable, and made pure by this very unattainability. Above all, it was proof of the superiority of the lover to those mere mortals who are capable of love only when it is returned.

Janis for the life of her could not see love as a commodity. It was a kind of spiritual essence that she jealously guarded lest it be contaminated by a fallen world.

Janis's songs became a sort of Love Court where the maligned prisoner of love could have her case heard by "witnesses." When she hit the stage at full tilt, the volatility of unspeakable emotion that took hold of her was overwhelming in its sheer, all-consuming energy. Janis was addressing the audience as her lover.

And Janis, in matters of love, would tolerate no indifference.

*With Paul Morrissey, Andy Warhol and Tim Buckley at Max's Kansas City,
New York, 1969* [ELLIOT LANDY]

an afternoon of serious drinking
(a little slice of real life for ya, folks!)

In felawschipe wel coude sche lawghe and carpe.
Of remydyes of love sche knew perchaunce,
For of that art sche knew the olde daunce.

Chaucer, *Prologue, The Canterbury Tales*

Janis: I've been down here *an hour and a half.* Boy, was I surprised. I thought I'd have to eat yogurt or something. What time do the bars open here? Eleven?

Mr. A: Ten

Janis: Now *that's* civilized!

Mr. A: Tomorrow the only thing you can get is beer.

Janis: I'll be in Kansas.

David: You look great today, Janis, almost, uh, *medieval.*

Janis: I look like I had a *good* night . . . .

David: Yeah, I'm sorry I missed that party, I, uh, got stoned and . . . .

Janis: Wasn't exactly a party, man. It was your usual after-the-gig-all-the-bands-in-the-same-motel goony bash. Not a single groupie in sight. I was the only chick there, and I couldn't get any action!

David: That's too bad.

Janis: No wonder I'm so pissed off.

BAR RAP #1

Mr. A: Johnny and I went down there and kicked Roger Miller's ass. Kicked his *ass,* I tell you!

Mr. B: Johnny who?

Mr. A: Johnny Cash, boy. You heard of Johnny Cash, now didn't you? He only happens to be *the* greatest singer in this goddamn country, at the present time.

Mr. B: Says you.

Mr. A: Hell, he can sing anything. Gospel, country, ballads, rock 'n' roll. You name it.

Mr. B: Soul.

Mr. A: What?

Mr. B: You asked me to name one thing he couldn't sing and I was tellin' ya I'd like to see Johnny Cash sing soul music.

Mr. A: Whatta ya talkin' about, he's got soul. You heard the album he and June Carter made in the Holy Land?

Mr. B: Nope. I must've missed that one.

Mr. A: It's about to be the most *soul*ful thing you *ever* heard.

Mr. B: Still, it ain't *soul* music, man. I'd like to hear him do "Hot Pants."

Mr. A: Who'd *want* to.

Mr. B: But that's my point, see?

David: It may not be soul, man, but he's still great.

Janis: Black and white, black and white! That's a little slice of real life for ya, folks! Let me tell ya what I think . . . . I saw his show, the Johnny Cash Show, one time, and I decided I wanted to be on it. You know, most shows are such shit, like selling plastic raindrops . . . and there's Johnny, he's staring into this thing, this multi-dimensional tube, talkin' about things that hurt him, things that hurt you. Just tellin' it like it is, man. Talkin' about the truth, man, and I was sitting there and all of a sudden I was sitting up, going "whew!" and the minute I got off, I called up the office and said, "Albert, Albert, get me on the show before that guy leaves." A lot of the segments are "hiya, folks!"good old Grand Ole Opry shit, but when he talks into that camera and says, "When I was sixteen, man, I this and I that . . . "—his eyes never leave yours. The effect is so real, you really feel this cat is talking to you, you know. I'd rather do that than the Ed Sullivan Show. I've done that, and it's bullshit, man.

BAR RAP #2

Janis: You work real hard and get to a certain point when you're accepted, and you sell out. You opt for an image. But . . . you can only sell out once! Well, far as I'm concerned, Tom Jones could've been a real heavy weight in the music biz. I mean he could've really *meant* something in the music biz. He's *that* talented. He sold out the minute they came to him, instead of letting his talent grow up. No, he opted real early. Too early!

Mr. A: There's the other side to the flip side of that coin.

Janis: Maybe I don't know what I'm talking about. Sold out five years too early.

Mr. A: So why not?

Janis: He's okay . . . watered down James Brown. But Tom Jones could've been the greatest singer in the world. He's got the talent. He could've been a *definitive* singer. What I mean is, he could've been Jimi Hendrix to the Pop World! Guts.

Mr. B: He's gettin' all the *money* in the world, right now.

Janis: So's Jimi Hendrix, man.

Mr. A: But he coulda got more. What're you gettin' these days?

Janis: I'm nickle 'n' diming it all the way. Sittin' here hustlin' drinks for it.

Mr. B: [*in all seriousness*] Don't say that too loud in here! People might get the wrong idea.

Mr. A: You don't hustle *screwdrivers*, fer Chrissakes!

Janis: I don't need to take any shit off you guys, I'm buying my own drinks. Anyway, I was just goofin' on ya.

BAR RAP #3

Mr. A: Hey, you *know* Tom Jones?

Janis: Yeah, I did a show with him. He's short.

David: Tom Jones is short?

Janis: My height, dear. He seemed about my height. He's got big shoulders and thinks he's butch. He's always coming on to these chicks in the show cause he's got a big fat old wife he's had for 15 years. So I took some of my heavy California girlfriends down to this show. I got some really nice dynamite chicks, just like me . . . .

Mr. A: *Dykes* like Janis?

Janis: Whaaat?

Mr. A: Dykes like Janis?

Janis: No, I didn't say that.

David: She didn't say that at all.

Janis: So, anyway . . . . We're all sittin' in back, drinkin' Ripple and goin' "hmmmm!" and he's walkin' around pullin' these games. He's chattin' up this chick violinist that's wearin' fifteen pairs of eyelashes, hair stiff as a board, little panty girdle ass, y'know, the kid's got pretty weird taste. I kept watchin' him, and he's talkin' like this: [*phony English accent*] "Well, hi *theah*, what's *your* name?" Doin' that old fifties shit. Finally, after the show, I caught up with him and I said, y'know what your problem is? I got you all figured out—I was drunk enough to say that—I said, you don't like to be with a woman. You just want to *conquer* one, just wanna talk her into it. Well, let me tell you that's not what's happening anymore, because *women*, believe it or not, like it as much as men, if not *more*.

Mr. B: More! more!

Janis: I said, let's face it, man, what you oughta do is try a hippie chick, because they know what they want and they *like it*, man. [*Welsh accent*] "Oh, I couldn't. Thank you." So I said, later for you, honey!

Mr. A: He's the *im*potent sex symbol.

Janis: Oh, he's probably potent, he's just still into that old macho thing. Although that's giving macho a bad name.

Mr. A: What you do is you scare 'em away. You're too scary.

Janis: But I'm not *all* hippie chicks. I said, try a hippie chick, I didn't say *me*, man. Because if they *dig* it, nothing scares them away. The concept that the chick might really know what she's doing and *want* it, that she might *dig* what she's doing is what scares *them*. They like that guilt-ridden, "I'm hurting you, I'm screwing you, I'm doing you wrong and I'm doing it with every strength in my will and my cock." It's a macho thing. Obviously.

Mr. A: But around here even the girl longhairs don't do that. You gotta unnerstan' where we're talkin'. This is Kentucky, fer Chrissake! This ain't no hippie commune!

Janis: Is that so?

Mr. A: Now, tell ya what I did. Twenty years of marriage, and I got up and walked out on it . . . .

Janis: On *it*?

Mr. A: The whole thing. And I got myself a roommate.

Janis: Male or female?

Mr. A: Female.

Janis: Those are the best kind.

Mr. A: I'm not a switch hitter. I'm *real* straight. But, see, my housemate allows me one night a week to get what I can on my own.

Janis: Get it while you can!

Mr. A: She says, "You can go out one night a week and get anything you can get your hands on." That makes her *lovely*.

Janis: Where do you think she is? And what do you think she's doing while you're out there gettin' it on?

Mr. A: If she can get it, if it makes her happy—that's fine.

Janis: I'll drink to that.

Mr. A: It doesn't bother me. Let her take whatever she can get.

Janis: No, man. Shall I tell you something I learned from a cat one time? I was busy talkin' about how this guy took me and then split on me. And then this cat who was my cat

said, "Lissen, babe, when someone gives it away, it's gone. Ain't nobody takes nothin' off you, man. It ain't a piece of pie." No chick ever takes a cat. As far as I'm concerned, we just use 'em. When you get through, you still got what you started out with, except you're feeling better.

Mr. B: Hit the box.

Janis: I'm not on the box.

Mr. A: You're not making it, lady.

["*Don't Let Me Down*" *is playing on the jukebox.*]

Janis: Don't let me down, *indeed!*

Mr. A: What's this that's playin'?

David: Don't bring me down . . . .

Janis: And don't put me down either or I'll kill ya. [*cackles*] Don't know why I go around saying that—I never hit anybody in my life, man.

BAR RAP #4

Mr. B: I'm one of the biggest patrons of this hotel and I didn't know you were coming in.

Janis: I'll tell you something, man, nobody in this place knows who the fuck I am—or cares. 80-year-old bartender doesn't give a shit. Has to serve me cause of the civil rights law, is all. I don't care. I was in a bar last week— tried to throw me out because the cat I was with didn't have a jacket. What it comes down to is they didn't want us there. Sat down had a drink, put down a hundred dollar bill and split. I *love* being able to do that. Didn't used to be able to, not so long ago. I used to plead, "Awh, c'mon, man!"

Mr. B: I want you to meet my wife . . . .

Janis: Can I make a point?

Mr. B: She don't want me to sing no more. I used to play with Johnny Taylor. I'm good.

Janis: No shit.

Mr. B: This my home, can't do nothin' here . . . . I'm 35 years old, unnerstan'?

Janis: He's older than me, can you dig it! [*cackles*]

Mr. B: So she say, "Al, you go on 'n' do your photography, get yourself together." One job. That's it. I bin travellin' all my life. Had a band, a bunch of smokin' records.

Janis: Turn that tape back. There's a point I wanted to make, it *was* very important, that was very important to me— it seemed.

Mr. B: You with her band?

David: No, I'm, uh . . . .

Mr. A: In residence. I'll write your lines for you, okay?

David: Actually, I'm from *Rolling Stone.*

Mr. B: You all played in Milwaukee one time?

David: No, I'm not Charlie Watts, unfortunately . . . .

Janis: It's a rock 'n' roll newspaper and he's writing a thing about me in the *Stone.*

David: I'd rather be with the Rolling Stones.

Janis: No, you wouldn't, honey. Now, *what* was I talkin' to you about? C'n you recall, honey?

Mr. B: See, I think I'm gonna buy me a farm. Not to farm it, y'unnerstan'. Just need about 15 acres, some horses. See, my wife, she's crazy about horses . . . .

Janis: Dear Lord! Regular bar conversation. I love bar conversation, man! There's four people talkin', nobody listening to anybody else, someone constantly offending, another cat constantly interrupting with a monologue about his car gettin' repossessed or some other matter of great import—"So I told that guy . . ."—and a third person constantly apologizing. This third cat is saying, "I'm really sorry about a minute ago that I" . . . . Talk about *cinéma vérité!* Drunks are all alike. Bitch, bitch, bitch, bitch, and every quarter of an hour they've got their arms around each other sayin', "I'm sorry, you're the greatest buddy I ever met."

Mr. A: You can always get lost, lady.

David: Hey, man, it'd be a crime for her to go away, she makes so many people happy . . . .

Janis: I'm not talkin' about that, man. I'm talkin' about

69

this, man: one to one confrontation. That's one thing I do not like—the star trip. I'm not trying to say, "I'm important, leave me alone." I'm talkin' about just one to one. I'm tryin' to say, "I'm buyin' my own drinks, you can't bother me." Those cats at the bar, man, tryin' to treat me funny cause my tits show, my feathers . . . .

Mr. A: Y'know, I'd like to see your tits . . . .

Janis: Eat your heart out! Eat your heart out! [to waitress] If you've got a check, I'll sign it. Maybe you got a bar tab?

Waitress: He already paid.

Janis: Ooooh, honey. You're such a sweetheart. Sure know how to make a girl feel good. [cackles] Wheee!

David: Ah, shucks . . . .

Janis: I pay for everything—cigarettes, booze. Nobody's ever got any money but me. And I figure I got more money than anybody else.

Mr. A: Hey, this all being recorded?

David: It doesn't matter if it's being recorded or not. It's happening.

Janis: Let's assume that both of our minds are hip enough to remember what you're saying, whether it's being recorded or not. In people confrontation, it just don't matter, man. Can you dig that? Get real, man. You can't be anything else.

Mr. A: Okay, can I have a cigarette and can I get in your pants?

Janis: Not this afternoon, I-don't-think.

David: Lay off, man. I'm saying that to *you.*

Mr. A: I'll tell you one thing, I ain't goin' home alone.

Janis: [wailing] Ooowwooowweee!

Mr. A: Now, you're sayin' you can go anywhere you want to? Do anything anytime, anyplace you're at?

Mr. B: It's a free country, man.

Janis: That's news to me!

David: *This is life!*

Mr. A: Still 'n' all.

70

Janis: Now I remember what I was sayin'. Talkin' about comin' in here and gettin' treated *mean*. Got treated rude and mean the moment I walk in this place.

Mr. B: But, darlin', you're the *cee-leb-rit-y!*

Janis: That's just people shit. It has nothing to do with your *role* and your occupation in *life*, mine being a popstar. Cause what does a popstar mean to an 80-year-old bartender. A flying fuck is what it means, y'know?

Mr. A: You're some kinda freak, is what you're sayin'?

David: Hey, *where* are you coming from, man?

Mr. A: I'm from New York.

David: Bullshit.

Mr. A: That's no way to talk to someone you're drinkin' buddies with.

David: People insult each other all the time in New York, or haven't you ever noticed?

Janis: Get down! Get down! [*cackles*] I love it!

Mr. B: Now, I could tell, when you ran my thing down for me, I knew you was some kinda guy that reads.

Janis: This is better than the Mets game. Oh boy, what a morning! [*cackles*]

Mr. B: But you, man, ya gotta unnerstan' these people down here. You're from New York, but down here is still in the eighteenth century.

Janis: I sat here for an hour and a half. Not a goddamn solitary person would talk to me. Couldn't throw me out, so the cats at the bar just sat and stared at me . . . .

Mr. A: I thought you was one of the hippies, y'know . . . .

Janis: I *am*.

Mr. A: Well, y'know, just some hippie girl. How's I to know you was Janis Joplin?

Janis: But that's just what I am, man, is a hippie chick. What I do for living has got fuck all to do with it.

David: I can vouch for it. I saw her three years ago singing from the back of a truck.

Mr. B: I saw ya sittin' there, too. But I'm black, man, can you dig it? And no black cat is gonna go over and hit on a white chick in a bar down here.

Janis: I'm not talkin' about *hittin'* on me, man . . . .

Mr. A: Know somethin'? You're one weird broad.

David: Look, she doesn't need to be hit on by her . . . uh . . . friends.

Janis: Matter of fact, I think I'm right *on*.

Mr. B: Would you like to meet my wife? Would you meet her?

Janis: Well . . . I'm not real fond of women . . . . [*cackles*]

Mr. A: Let me guess , . . she's white.

Janis: What'sa matter, man, can't you take it?

Mr. A [*to Mr.B*]: Lissen, I'm not ready to meet *you* yet.

Mr. B: You're right about that!

David: You *gotta* get ready, like the gospel says.

Mr. B: We're all gonna be there [*singing*] "On that train . . . ."

Janis: I do the best I can. Better than bein' bored, right? Better than feelin' like a failure in Louisville, Kentucky.

Mr. B: We—what's your name?

David: Janis. Janis Joplin.

Mr. B: We just got off our honeymoon three weeks ago.

Janis: Sure, I'd love to meet your wife.

Mr. A: I'd be proud to meet your wife.

Janis: Tell her to get her ass down here and I'll buy her a drink.

Mr. A: Don't talk like that, I got my girl's picture in my pocket.

Janis: [*The waitress whispers something to Janis and she shrieks.*] You won't believe what she just told me! [*more cackling*] You're not gonna believe this. Our waitress just told me the fi*lthiest* joke. She just whispered in my ear: "Did you hear about the girl that took a douche with LSD, alum and Colonel Sanders chicken?" "No," I said, "I didn't." She said, "It was uptight, outta sight and finger-lickin' good!" [*cackles*] The South, baby.

Mr. B: My nephew, course he's workin' today, but he can play the guitar better'n you ever heard. Plays a real funky bass too . . . .

Janis: This gonna be one of those absolutely insane, uncontrollable bar conversations.

David: I'm into reality, Janis, and I love you.

Janis: You're supposed to be doin' an article on me, man. fuck reality!

SOUTHERN
TALES

I believe that phantasms are nothing but a little unbalanced condition of our mind: images that we fail to hold within the boundaries of the kingdom of sleep. They appear even in the daytime; and they terrify. I am greatly frightened when at nighttime I see them before me—disorderly images that, having dismounted from their horses, laugh. I am sometimes afraid, even of my blood that throbs in my veins like the thud of steps resounding in distant rooms in the silence of the night.

Pirandello, *Henry IV*

waking dreams

elow there is nothing. Only an amorphous white element sealing us off from the world beneath, the rain pitting the translucent geography of the airplane window where minuscule rivers begin and end in the twinkling of an eye.

Janis is reading, swimming off into a firmament of her own, burrowing into the leaves of *Zelda*. Its jacket is a nest of flamelike peacock feathers that glow in Janis's ringed hands, looking more like a chunky bouquet than a book. Janis reads a lot, and these books (*Tender Is The Night, Look Homeward, Angel, The Crack-Up*) that she lugs about with her on her journeys have a curious effect, almost approaching possession, their words and images pollinating her life with waking dreams.

Perhaps fortunately for Janis, all this reading, absorption and general intellectual turn of mind did not intrude on her singing and songwriting, which always remained very basic, gutsy, immediate and devoid of reflection. Her considerable intelligence, in fact, did not prevent her from creating some of the brassiest, most deliciously corny lyrics imaginable.

But in the quiet hours—backstage, on planes, at airports and in all the vacant moments of life on the road—the tiny roots of empathy reach out of the pages and embed themselves in her mind's eye, infusing her daydreams with the traces of fine summery afternoons and sultry evenings of sixty years ago.

Are you digging it?

The book or Zelda? I'm not crazy about the book, man,

but her life, man, that is something else. She was as fucking crazy as I am. I was just reading about how she was at this dance, and afterwards in her velvet gown and carrying a bouquet of roses—you wouldn't believe how romantic her whole thing is, course it was a very romantic time—anyway she's coming back from this dance and she's passing this photography shop that has a photograph of one of Zelda's beaus in the window. This chick that's with her makes some dumb remark about how he ought to be with her rather than being in the shop window. So you know what she does, man? She kicks in the glass right there and takes out his photograph and walks away bold as brass with it and takes it to this cafe with her just like she was on a date. I mean she was *real* crazy, you know?

Didn't she flip out in the end?

Yeah. Well, that was a lot later. She wrote these heartrending letters to Scott. She was in a lot of institutions. I think everything that happened to her was just too much in the end. What I'm trying to say is that she had all these romantic aspirations and stuff and they all *really* happened to her eventually. So what I think is that that just freaked her out, it's like having a dream about something and then it actually happens.

From letters Zelda wrote to Fitzgerald from Dr. Forel's clinic:
Dear Scott,

. . . I want to get well but I can't it seems to me, and if I should what's going to take away the thing in my head that sees so clearly into the past and into dozens of things that I can never forget. Dancing has gone and I'm weak and feeble and I can't understand why I should be the one, amongst all others, to have to bear all this—for what . . . ?

Yesterday, I had some gramophone discs that reminded me of Ellerslie. I wonder why we have never been very happy and why all of this has happpened—it was much nicer a long time ago when we had each other and the space about the world was warm—Can't we get it back someway—even by imagining . . . ?

Janis immersed in The Submariner; *Dave Getz contemplates*
The Growing Drug Abuse [ELLIOT LANDY]

Janis opens *Zelda* to the center of the book where there are photographs of her and Scott, old snapshots and drawings, the comings and goings of a life. Zelda in ballet costume—ruffles of tulle and ribbon encircle her like a precocious flower.

In a little picture entitled "Folly" she is sitting in a field of flowers as if she'd just sprung up. Janis is as familiar with all these hieroglyphs of Zelda's life as she might be of her own. She seems to bounce off the photographs as if they were little gray mirrors. Here's a drawing by Ring Lardner of Zelda that's been glued onto an old newspaper clipping. She is dressed in a winky Petty-girl coat as she steps onto this unexplained ledge of question marks. A following page contains a more gloomy image ominously entitled "Recovered." The oscillating, staring eyes, barely able to contain the madness behind them, glare out of a tensely drawn face framed by a short institutional haircut.

What happened before and after these moments, an afternoon in the middle of a field in 1916? They are as enigmatic as any photos we now have of Janis. Janis is both envious of Zelda and fascinated by this wild Southern girl whose romantic mother named her after a gypsy queen in a sentimental novel.

Janis glumly points out the last photograph of Zelda in the book. Appropriately, she is standing rather stiffly in the bucket of a huge crane as if about to be lifted off the earth.

"How our love shone through any old trite phrase in a telegram," Scott wrote in one of his jottings collected in *The Crack-Up*. There is a photograph of Zelda's scrapbook where these cables from Scott are pasted like little white clouds with devotional care.

Growing up in the Deep South had a lot to do with the concreteness of Janis's vision of herself because the South, with its ruminant, brittle quality—like Tennessee Williams's vulnerable romantic women whom Janis also resembles—seems to hoard up time, relatively sheltered as it is from the changes of a more fluid society.

Janis also shared with Zelda the almost literary tenets of Southern womanhood, the spirited veneer of the legendary Southern belle with its attendant charades of etiquette and morality that are still a facet of life in the Deep South. They both grew up in this claustrophobic atmosphere with its elaborate anachronistic modes of proper behavior that unconsciously support a delicious irony: well brought up Southern girls grow up under similar halters of tradition and confining social restrictions as the Southern black. It was, perhaps, this perverse affinity that gave such credence to Janis's blues.

Both willful, headstrong girls, who were at the same time sensitive enough to appreciate the lush romantic tradition they grew up with, Janis and Zelda were torn between wanting to tear down all the silly pretenses of this feudal society (with its faint echoes of Sir Walter Scott tiptoeing about Tara) and living gracefully within its many privileges. Such a conflict had one day driven Zelda to write: ". . . it's very difficult to be two simple people at once, one who wants to have a law to itself and another who wants to keep all the nice old things and be loved and safe and protected."

How did you come to get into this strong identification thing with Zelda?

I always did have a very heavy attachment for the whole Fitzgerald thing, that all out, full tilt, hell bent way of living, and she and F. Scott Fitzgerald were the epitome of that whole trip, right? When I was young I read all of his books. I've reread them all, autobiographies, *The Crack-Up*, all the little scribblings . . . and she was always a mythic person in his life, you also have the feeling that he destroyed her, you always get the feeling that she was willing to go with him through *anything*, and that he ruined her. But in the book you find out that she was just as ambitious as he was, and that they sort of destroyed each other. He wrote her a letter one time in which he says, "People say we destroy each other, but I never felt we destroyed each other. I felt we destroyed ourselves."

Why are you so attracted to them?

Are you trying to find out if I identify with them?

Yeah.

Yes, of course, I do. That's obvious. We've got sort of the same trip going. But she was luckier, she had him. She found a part of herself. But I do not think that the end she came to is necessarily a product of that. It seemed to be more because of her thwarted ambition and her Southern childhood that dropped her. But I haven't finished the book yet. Oh my God, she had such a beautiful way with words. . . . Fitzgerald took a lot of things from her, lifted things from her diary. She was every one of his female characters—Nicole Diver, the charming woman, she was all of them. She wrote, too, but he would take her stories and publish them under his own name. That was their deal. Anything she wrote or said, he got to use it in his work. She was a very romantic character and I have a very high sense of the romantic, as you may have noticed.

Yeah, I've noticed you're into that twenties and thirties type of thing.

I'm an anachronism, that's what it is.

How did you get that way?

I don't know, man. I mean I'm not a 1930's anything; I'm just a fifties chick, but I suppose my thoughts and fantasies go to that more expansive, more abandoned time, you know? Not those coy games people like to play, not like the little flirt games, you know. More like, "Well, boys?" Doesn't seem to be doing me too much good either. But, you know, they'll all come around!

Do you identify with Mae West then?

Oh, yeah. She's dynamite, but, uh, I think I have too much insecurity . . . reality and humanness . . . I could never, I mean I may say it, but I don't mean it. I don't know her well enough to know whether she means it or not either. I think she probably even *means* it. I can pull it off, you know . . . but anybody that knows me knows . . . . But I like that style. I like that way of living. I like that way of looking at things. It's down to gut level, man. The truth, man. It's *down*. I'm hungry, feed me, make me happy . . . . [*In a throaty whisper*] Come here . . . whoooo!

Parasites descending out of time fall on the exposed and innocent. They often choose as their victims the naive, and all those with a nostalgia for paradise in their eyes. Janis was one of those naive people. Being naive has nothing to do with how much you know or read, it is expecting things to happen against all the obvious indications, expecting things will turn out all right in the end.

Zelda, Bessie, Billie and Nicole Diver were her immaterial doubles, cores which Janis reached by intoxicating herself with their lives. Possession induced by fantasies. Janis's flirtation with these departed spirits was a very real traffic with "let's pretend," enticing all the beautiful, silky, seductive shades that reach out with their fatal tendrils to attach themselves to the living.

Janis's restlessness came from the static of all these voices, the ceaseless chatter of those who inhabit the possessed and make it impossible for them to live their lives simply. At every moment a host of presences is moving under the surface with its mass of unlived lives.

The impersonations (putting on Bessie for the blues) were not simply representations but very *real* identifications. They went beyond and preceded her knowledge. Janis was already living out pieces of Zelda's life before she knew who Zelda was.

These spirits lie in wait in images, words and songs, they wait for the accidentally left open window to the past. They fly in at the brain. In daydreams they take possession of us. We give them shelter by expelling the more trivial aspects of ourselves. Obsessed with history and the tailing of exemplary lives, we march in parades of lost souls, who revive when we listen. Is it this that gives rise to those truisms that the recently departed always elicit?

Saxophonist Martin Fierro, playing with Quicksilver on the night Janis died: "She's here tonight, man, you know what I mean? She's in everybody's hearts, mouths, and heads. Everybody says, 'I wish she's here.' She's in my heart, man, screaming . . . laughing . . . bitching, man, bitching."

Images infest the living everywhere—in songs, in words, in old pictures from a remote time. For Janis, it was the twenties, crystal, intangible, and silent except for the voices that she gave them.

east of eden

> Americans, he liked to say, should be born with fins, and perhaps they were—perhaps money was a form of fin. In England, property begot a strong place sense, but Americans, restless and with shallow roots, needed fins and wings. There was even a recurrent idea in America about an education that would leave out history and the past, that should be a sort of equipment for aerial adventure, weighted down by none of the stowaways of inheritance or tradition.
>
> F. Scott Fitzgerald, *The Crack-Up*

Janis knew that when people talked about "Janis" they were talking about the mythical Janis that *Cashbox* called a "kind of mixture of Leadbelly, a steam engine, Calamity Jane, Bessie Smith, an oil derrick and rotgut bourbon, funneled into the 20th century somewhere between El Paso and San Francisco."

It was easy to pick up on this side only. It was the Janis everybody always talked about—the mind's eye Janis, gutsy, ballsy, funky—and it was also the easiest Janis to write about. It was, predictably, the only Janis that ever got into print. There was nothing enigmatic or ambivalent about it. Janis barreling into town, trading raunchy stories with the boys, setting up drinks. It was so put together. Small town journalists in the South and Midwest lapped it up, a bit of color in between the announcements. They were just witnesses to a good performance.

But Janis was no low riding rube from a high-grass town. She was brought up in cities—Port Arthur, Austin—with all the predictable certainties of middle-class American life. These didn't change much from one state to another, bound together as they were by the insidious cohesions of *Life* magazine, Ozzie and Harriet, Kleenex, Coca-Cola, Perry Como, and the *Saturday Evening Post.* It was an act of will and supreme imagination on Janis's part to sustain the illusion of that *child's dream of space* through which she realized herself.

You could actually see the traces of all these places–Kokomo, East Helena, the South Side of Chicago—and all the people she had never known but who had nevertheless grown into her: the whole childhood of America—endless spaces, wagons, frontiers, the iron horse, the restlessness of purpose in the promised land, impossible longings, *aerial adventures.* Freedom itself seemed to be an inheritance. Janis was an "American value," as Gerald Fitzgerald (Scott's brother) had said of Zelda.

Janis called herself a deliberate, contrived anachronism. She was an American beauty, grown ripe on memories of a romantic, heroic, industrious Eden. It is a pure, elemental vision that still lingers on California citrus labels, the vanished mirage of America.

Below, the real landscape has reappeared, the mist drifting away suddenly like an atlas opened to Kentucky. The stage for the afternoon is being set. Ladies and gentlemen, on your right is the Ohio River, played this afternoon by the letter S. The patches slide by below, yellow, red, brown, as articulately spaced as regional areas in a geography book, where each color knows its order. Flipping the pages of Kentucky, Louisville dramatically appears in due course in the form of the letter T, like a letter dropped from a giant alphabet, extending its arms nine miles along the Ohio River, its tail curling up into the hills.

"i'm saving the bass player for omaha"

Full Tilt Boogie were a strange group in relation to Janis. With the exception of Clark Pierson, all were almost a decade younger than Janis, and she treated them with the maternal solicitousness of an aroused stepmother.

Although they weren't as intimate as Big Brother, who had resembled a real family with all the turbulence of unconditioned ups and downs, Full Tilt nevertheless had none of the session player anonymity of Janis's second band, Kozmic Blues. The tangible affection that flowed between Full Tilt and Janis showed itself in the playfulness they generated on stage. A weird combination, too. Earthy, jaded, outrageous Janis, and Full Tilt, who for the most part were quiet and introspective and (by comparison) innocent.

But the quiet, inward qualities of Full Tilt were a perfect foil for Janis, and she stood out in brilliant relief against their muted personalities, somewhat like the Midnight Special panting down the track must have stood out against a moonlit night.

The band had a certain dignity about them, emanating in part from John Cooke, possibly the most urbane road manager in all rock. In his cowboy trophies from Miller's Western Outfitters in Denver, he looked like the last city marshal from Cambridge, Mass.

On tour, only Clark's raucous voice would compete with Janis's in the muffled hum of planes, coming on in its best Dodge City manner to some rinsed-out blonde.

Sometimes, like when an R. Crumb special came jiggling her beebite boobies down the aisle, stuffed into a pair of faded jeans, Janis, feeling their reticence insulted the self-respect of red-blooded American womanhood, would alert "the boys" with a loud "BING-GO!"

John is reading a chronicle of the Kiowa Indians. His fantasy America is further back in time than Janis's, back "beyond the rolling hills of the Republic." Injuns, Army scouts, and Lewis and Clark; the tantalizing secrets of the frontier.

Brad Campbell is smiling—at some interior joke—with that innocent, vacant *Hee-Haw* grin on his face. Richard Bell taps his spooky harmonies on a silent piano while Ken Pearson and John Till, wired with headphones to their private universe, trade tapes of Coltrane, King Biscuit Boy, and Lambert, Hendricks and Ross.

"Basically, we're like studio musicians who were put together for a session," Ken Pearson, the organist, explains with his characteristic modesty. "It's not like we played together in the garage for three years before making it. We're still finding out what kind of music we like. I'll go over to John's room and he'll play me something and I'll say, 'You mean, you like *that?*' You know, we're just a group of musicians from really different backgrounds, thrown together, slowly becoming a family."

Ken himself worked with a lot of small rock and jazz bands in Canada. He backed up folk singer Ronny Abramson and played with Penny Lang's Montreal Symphony 1500 before joining Jesse Winchester about a year ago as a piano player. Jesse had come north to avoid the draft and had planned to head west with his four-man band in an old bus, just stopping and doing a number wherever they happened to be, when Robbie Robertson offered to record him. Robbie had got together a bass player and a drummer for the session, but still needed a keyboard, so Jesse and Ken were the only members of the original group to play on the album. Ken would probably have stayed with Jesse's band, but when Jesse was billed to play a gig in February of 1970 with the Band, Jesse felt his group would provide a better contrast to the Band's full sound if he played with just himself and a bass player. So Ken was temporarily out of a job. It was just at this time that Janis was looking to form a new backup group.

Although Janis says that one of the reasons she left the second group was that she was always fighting the volume of the horns, she misses the punch that horns give her. "They gave me that *umph* when I needed it." But it's unlikely that her audience will miss them. John Till's lead guitar and Ken Pearson's organ fill in beautifully where the horn lines were, and they are a better harmonic match for Janis's voice.

When Janis left Big Brother, it was like a marriage that had broken up, and ever since that time she had been looking for a partner that had the virtues of spontaneity and freshness without being amateurish. Her new group comes as close to that as time allowed. If they are not quite what Big Brother was to Janis, it is perhaps because they were not part of the original Panhandle Park mythology. But as musicians they're more together than Big Brother. Also, Janis relates to them. "These guys are on the same wavelength as me," Janis says, "it's more of a family thing again."

John Till (lead) and Brad Campbell (bass) are the only two members Janis took with her from the last band. Brad had been with the second band since the beginning, but John joined Janis toward the end, playing rhythm guitar. He's a subtle and fast blues guitarist who started with Ronnie Hawkins's band three years ago straight out of high school.

"Ronnie likes to get you real young and brainwash you. He'll make you think you couldn't play with anyone else even if you wanted to, and then he puts you in a black suit and a store-bought haircut, and you just stay there until you've got the guts to pull out." Brad, who played bass in the last group, comes from the now defunct Paupers (also managed by Albert Grossman) where he replaced Danny Gerard, and his bass is a solid match for Clark Pierson's drumming.

Richard Bell (piano) also comes from Ronnie Hawkins's band and both he and John Till backed the legendary Canadian harp player and singer King Biscuit Boy, otherwise known as

Richard Newall. Bell's piano is both honky-tonky and jazzy and is a light improvisational element in a group that is heavily rhythmic. Richard was in college when Hawkins offered him "$50 a week and his laundry" and gave him 30 seconds to make up his mind. He took it. For all the weird stories attached to his name, Ronnie Hawkins, like a Canadian John Mayall, seems to have attracted and developed a number of really talented musicians.

All the members of Full Tilt are Canadians, except for Clark Pierson who played drums with Linn County. Janis discovered Clark playing in the house band of the Galaxy, a San Francisco topless club. His drumming has a funky, heavy bump and grind beat, a perfect match for Janis's raunchy voice. "You know, I've had drummers that used to go a-one, a-two, a-three . . ." says Janis. "Clark just slams right into it.

"They just weren't happening for me," Janis said the Kozmic Blues band. "They just didn't get me off. You know, I have to have the *umph*. I've got to *feel* it, because if it's not getting through to me, the audience sure as hell aren't going to feel it either. This band is solid, their sound is so heavy you could lean on it, and that means I can go further out and extend myself. It's together, man, that's what it is!"

David Dalton,
"Janis Joplin's Full Tilt Boogie Ride,"
Rolling Stone, August 6, 1970

thy alabaster cities gleam, undimmed by human tears

Airports always look desolate in spite of the crowds. This, I suppose, contributes to the profoundly dislocating sensation involved in travelling by air across America. In the *illusion* of travelling, I should say, because essentially everywhere is the same for the superficial traveller. His adventures are hardly likely to be revealing. This disagreeable disenchantment comes from the horrible realization that you are tunneling from one vacuum to another. On the surface, every city seems a replica of the previous one, as if some city-hungry mantis had been there just before you, leaving behind only a lifeless husk.

Arriving in Kansas City or Memphis, you wonder where the slinky riverboat ports and bawdy frontier towns of America have gone. You listen pointlessly for their breath and realize, a little remorsefully, that these historical behemoths who once roamed our continent, massive as bison, have been reduced to dull, sluggish sows by Circe's technocratic wand.

The airport is unmoved even by the bizarre band passing through its intestines. It greets us, as it does every new arrival, with the mindless cheerfulness of a freshly scrubbed corpse. Everything here is a mischievous illusion, a twilight zone hoax, and yet the terrible irony that all of this has been very deliberately constructed remains. In its own way, it is a miracle of American ingenuity and efficiency. It must be reassuring to someone. But to whom?

The Avis girl smiles at us predictably as John Cooke gets the transportation together. The rest of us moon about like zombies in the white, blank waiting areas, sliding along the finely polished funerary floors.

Only Janis knows what to do with the time, plunks herself down, uncorks a bottle and blatantly sucks away on it to the amazed glares of the surrounding businessmen and several pathetic straggling family groups.

In this context, Janis suddenly seemed gargantuan, profoundly real. She loomed among the shifting shades with a majestic density of being, as if she were descended from an almost extinct race of giants. Janis had this quality of making people disappear by comparison with her, a quality that, while necessary to her own psychic equilibrium, could be crushing to outsiders. Her ballsiness, of course, and tough, gin-mama contortions did well to sheathe a brittle, vulnerable core.

These collisions with the natives were often theatrical, even farcical, because Janis made everywhere she was her own stage and if you stepped onto the boards you were obliged to perform. Sometimes, however, these scenes were a little less than funny. The greatest possible insult, after all, is to question someone else's reality—something Janis did instinctively under hostile conditions. Her presence seemed to corrode everything other people took for granted, and for this reason most of the pointing, giggling impromptu audience kept their distance. For them, exposure to Janis had the disturbing effect of seeing an anti-matter particle of themselves oscillating wildly in dangerous proximity. To approach too closely meant risking some kind of personal detonation.

She represented everything they hated and weren't allowed to be, curled into a saucy ball of insolence. She scooped up all the hidden, grubby trash that had accumulated in their airless domes and shoved it at them like a huge smell. She created such catastrophic interferences and voids that her "victims" were bound to seek revenge. The crowning outrage was that she was not only fucking them, she was doing it in broad daylight, and the indiscretion seemed all the more flagrant in these immaculate spaces.

Janis was, for the most part, oblivious to their rays, because she carried around a private world into which she could retire. Amid all the indigestible flux of these places, she would plump herself down, as ripe as a pear in August, singing snatches of old songs to herself—personal incantations to ward off the environment, a bane against accumulated apprehensions. Usually they were not the kind of things she'd sing on stage— Merle Haggard, old Bessie Smith numbers, and her favorite, a formless ditty called, *It's Life*, which didn't have the slightest connection with Sinatra's ice cream sundae.

> *What's life?*
> *A magazine.*
> *How much does it cost?*
> *It only costs a quarter.*
> *A quarter? I've only got a nickel.*
> *That's life . . . .*

A bedbug in our synthetic universe, Janis was Mother Courage barreling through hell with her wagonload of goodies and sons tagging along behind: "If only we could find some peace and quiet where there's no shooting going on, me and my kids, what's left of 'em—we could rest up for a while."

In the airport bar, an officer from the local Shriners' convention—identicard pinned to lapel and decked out like the Garden of Allah—lunges at Janis like a dog appraising a building: "Hey, baby, you turned into a turtle yet?"

Janis looks defiantly into his cold blue Donald Duck eyes: "When I want you in my pond, asshole, I'll let you know."

Later, I naively ask Janis if he'd been talking about "Turtle Blues." "No, man," she says. "He was just being jive. He was just trying to be a smart ass. A lot of people do that. They'll challenge you once to see if you've got the balls to look like that. And, you know, if you go, 'Oooh, I'm sorry . . . uh, weel . . . egad . . .'—you know you're shot down already."

"i'm just a turtle that's hiding underneath its horny shell"

It is perfectly true, as the philosophers say, that life must be understood backwards. But they forget the other proposition, that it must be lived forwards. And if one thinks over that proposition it becomes more and more evident that life can never be understood in time simply because at no particular moment can one find the necessary resting place from which to understand it—backwards.

Kierkegaard, *Journals, 1843*

In the long hours that precede the show few things relieve the monotony. We are in a drab high-ceilinged dressing room with one bare light bulb. Janis is making faces at herself in the mirror. Time is mainly spent stringing her beads. Great Mother Weaver of the World at her endless task. Oddly shaped pieces of glass and stone, slipping knots, tying off loose ends. Each strand represents hours and days of boredom, waiting . . . waiting, passing of time. Each stone an hour, each knot a minute eaten up. The language of detached fingers emptied of thoughts, automatic, repetitious.

Then, with all its incredible formality, comes the ritual of the bracelets. The procedure is almost Tunisian in its intensity. Their elaborate shining rings glint in the harsh light of the tiny cubicle like the host of white birds that flew up after the birth of Cuchulainn, each with a silver yoke between them. The weight of all that ripe amber and silver metal! It must feel like carrying a spare arm around. Tinkling circles overlapping, crowding, burying each other. It's hard to believe they don't serve some religious function. Janis slips each one on deliberately, like feathery thin armor, and steps nightly into her own arena. It's not that the audience are cannibals, although in a sense they are that too, because the battle is really fought for them—with them—against all the dull, wrongheaded spectres that have cropped up during the day.

The performance is illusory, and the relief she will give them, like the yearly flight of the queen bee, is only a momentary ecstacy. But this frenzied meeting and hum of weightlessness is something that Janis needs too; the conspiracy is mutual, otherwise the repetitions would be murderous. Every night the same pretense at paradise, the same whirring ascension, the intoxication lingering a little before its predictible sinking back into grim little banalities. The conditions of this act fall on both sides—Janis, too, must return to earth.

During these endless hours Janis occasionally reminisces. But somehow the histories reveal only the itinerary of her myth. She does not consciously hide the secret places, yet a habit protects her. You have the feeling that her childhood is hidden even from herself, and that we are permitted to see her life only as a geologic fault. From the one side, from her parents, a certain kind of truth emerges, more hoped for and projected than perceived, and from our side we see only what has *become* of Janis, the monument stained by events, but in a sense more real, more focused than any life could actually be. The evolution of a star, her own program. What the components of this myth really are is a matter of indifference. As time passes we will leave its soft, amorphous outline further and further behind. This is as Janis would have wished it.

The truth is that the *facts* of a life that we pursue with missionary zeal are only signals from the great wastes. Our responses can only echo hollowly through these diffused experiences. Eventually we are forced to see the point. Janis is not dealing in random signals. A signal, a fact, a scratch on the field of time is a reduction, a mere resonance of the monotonous physical universe. If anything, Janis wanted her life to be read in *meanings*, a world of symbols in opposition to a world of noise.

The historical reality is unimportant. Janis spent her whole life erasing herself on this level, replacing it with myth. The actual memories of the events call across this giant fissure of time and space like the voices calling to each other across the river at the end of *La Dolce Vita*.

waller creek days

Can we talk about the past, Janis?
Past, yes, past.
How did Chet Helms find you?

I was in a hillbilly band, mostly hanging out—I was supposed to be going to college, but I just went up there so I could get it on. I was singing in this hillbilly group called the Waller Creek Boys, Waller Creek runs right through Austin, and Powell St. John was in the group, and a young guy called Lanny Williams who got married and had babies.

We used to sing at this place called the Ghetto and just hang out and get drunk a lot, get in big fights, roll in the mud, drink beer and sing, pick and sing, pick and sing. Walked around carrying my autoharp. Never went anywhere without my autoharp.

We were singing at this bar called Threadgill's on the outskirts of town. It was a converted gas station, it still had that awning and everything, you'd pull the car in and go in and have a beer, and Mr. Threadgill was a hillbilly singer. Every Saturday night everybody would go there. It was a very strange amalgam of people. There were all these old Okies, all the kids, little grandkids. Then there were a bunch of college professors—older cats that were into country music intellectually—the first of the folk trend, and then there were the young upstarts that were into it, too, and that was us.

And there was Mr. Threadgill—he surpassed them all. He was old, a great big man with a big belly and white hair combed back on the top of his head. And he was back there dishin' out Polish sausages and hard-boiled eggs and Grand Prize and Lone Star, "another eighteen Lone Star," dishin' out the Lone Star. And someone would say, "Mr. Threadgill, Mr. Threadgill, come out and do us a tune." And he'd say, "No, I don't think so," and they'd say, "Come on, come on," and he'd say, "All right." He'd close the bar down, and then he'd walk out front, and he'd lay his hands across his big fat belly, which was covered with a bar apron, just like in Duffy's Tavern. He'd come out like that and lean his head back and sing, just like a bird, Jimmie Rodgers songs, and he could yodel—God, he was fantastic!

We used to go there and sing every Saturday, and I was the young upstart loudmouthed chick—"That girl sounds a lot like Rosie Maddox, don't she?" And I'd sing Rosie Maddox songs, and I'd sing Woody Guthrie songs, but one time an evening I'd say, "Can I do one now? Can I do one now?" and they'd say, "Okay, let that lady have a tune," and I'd say, "Give me a 12 bar in E." I sang blues, I could only sing one a night . . . made it there every night!

Chet Helms heard me one weekend up there. He was famous, he was one of the crazies that made it away from Texas at a very early age, he had split at eighteen. He was back in town, on the way to the West Coast from the East Coast— all Texans come back to Austin—and he heard me singing. He said, "That girl's good, that girl's good."

I was wanting to leave, I was wanting to get the fuck out of there, but I didn't have quite enough nerve to leave by myself. Chet was leaving, and he said he wanted me to come with him, help him get rides. We hitchhiked to San Francisco, and we slept on a bunch of people's floors, and I sang a couple of times.

I wasn't really that interested in singing, to tell you the truth. I had a couple of opportunities, I just wasn't that serious about *anything*. I was just a young chick, I just wanted to *get it on*!

I wanted to smoke dope, take dope, lick dope, suck dope, fuck dope, anything I could lay my hands on I wanted to do it, man. Singing, singing just sort of faded out of my life, and I went through a number of personal changes, drug problems, heavy drug problems, and ended up back in Texas trying to get myself together, and I couldn't stand it down there. But I was afraid if I came back here I'd get fucked up again. I had been down there about a year, which was just enough time for me to get really sick of it.

How I really got in the band was really funny, it was perfectly apropos, because I hadn't been laid in a year, man, because who are you going to fuck in Port Arthur? I was down

With Chet Helms, San Francisco, 1967 [HERB GREENE]

there trying to kick, not getting fucked, trying to get through college because my mother wanted me to. I was in Austin doing a little folk music gig, playing the guitar, and this old boy friend of mine came—this cat I used to make it with—this was years after I left Austin, it was '65, I left in '61. I had gone to the big city and got good 'n' evil and came back home for a little R and R, right? This cat came down to where I was playing a gig. After the gig I was over at some people's house and I was sitting there and this cat came in and *scooped* me right up, man, it was Travis Rivers. He just came, and *scooped* me up, and threw me onto the bed, whoo, baby! He just fucked the livin' shit out of me all night long! Fucked me all night, fucked me all morning. I was feeling *sooo* good— you know how chicks are in the morning—a copout.

[*high chick's voice*] "Well, hi!"

[*low man's voice*] "What is it? Go get your clothes, I think we're going to California."

I just said, "Okay," but halfway through New Mexico I realized I'd been conned into being in the rock business by this guy that was such a good ball. I said, "Well, it's bound to be, man." I was fucked into being in Big Brother. But after I got here and started singing, I really loved it.

So I got to San Francisco and met all these strange guys. Chet knew me, and Chet was managing Big Brother. Chet had sent Travis down to try and talk me into being the center of his group, because he thought I was a good singer and would make it, but I had never gotten it together. He happened to hit me at the right time, and I came out to be in a group, but I didn't know it.

While I was gone, and I'd been in Texas for a long time, George Hunter was putting a show together. There was no rock 'n' roll in those days—it was '64 when I left—George was talking about putting me in a rock 'n' roll band. He had this poster, the first rock and roll poster. George drew it, and it said, "The Amazing Charlatans." I used to have it on my wall and go, "Far out, what have these crazy boys done now?"

I came back to San Francisco and rock 'n' roll had happened. Well, I'd never sung rock 'n' roll, I sang blues—Bessie Smith kind of blues. They said, "Janis, we want you to sing with these boys," and I met them all, and you know how it is when you meet someone, you don't even remember what they look like you're so spaced by what's happening. I was in space city, man, I was scared to death. I didn't know how to sing the stuff, I'd never sung with electric music, I'd never sung with drums, I only sang with one guitar. I'd learned "Down On Me." It's a gospel song, and I'd heard it before and thought I could sing it, and they did the chords. So we practiced it all week, and they were working at the Avalon that weekend. They played a few numbers, and then they said, "Now we'd like to introduce . . ."

And nobody had ever heard of fuckin' me, I was just some chick, didn't have any hip clothes or nothing like that. I had on what I was wearing to college. I got on stage, and I started singing, whew! what a rush, man! A real, live, drug rush. I don't remember it at all, all I remember is the sensation—what a fuckin' gas, man. The music was boom, boom, boom! and the people were all dancing, and the lights, and I was standing up there singing into this microphone and getting it on, and whew! I dug it. So I said, "I think I'll stay, boys." Far out, isn't it? It sure did take *me* by surprise, I'll tell you. I wasn't planning any of this, I wasn't planning on sittin' in cold dressing rooms all my life, I didn't even know it existed.

Even once I was a singer, I never wanted to be a star. I just liked to sing because it was fun, just like people like to play tennis, it makes your body feel good. Everybody gave you free beer. I don't remember much of the early period, we just worked around, all of us starving, I got some money from my parents . . . .

I could've met Otis Redding twenty times and married him, but once I saw him on a stage . . . he's a star, man! I've never been that close to a star.

You're a star, Janis.

That's different . . . and besides, I haven't accepted that kind of thing yet. You can't *say* you're a star. I know me, I've been around a long time, I've been this chick for twelve, thirteen years now. I was younger then, more inexperienced, but I was the same person with the same drives and the same balls and the same style.

I was the same chick, because I've been her forever, and I know her, and she ain't no star: she's lonely, or she's good at something. I have to get undressed after the show, my clothes are ruined, my heels are run through, my underwear is ripped, my body's stained from my clothes, my hair's stringy, I got a headache and I got to go home, and I'm lonely, and my clothes are all fucked up, my shoes have come apart, and I'm pleading with my road manager to please give me a ride home, please, please, just so I can take these fuckin' clothes off, and that ain't no star, man, that's just a person.

I have one thing I can do, and I'm gettin' better at it, too, which makes me feel like an artist rather than a fluke, man, which I think I was. I just happened to have the right combination at the right time. But now I am learning how, and that's my job, to improve, and I am, and that makes me feel good. Everybody can do something at some time, but people aren't interested in what one person can do, and pass by and always be a loser, but in another place and time they just may come to you, and that doesn't mean you're any better than anybody else. So many people don't try. I mean there are people who really fuckin' try to be fair and to be good at what they do, they really fucking work, they're artists, in artistic bands, they really try.

But I was just lucky, and I know how lucky I am, because I've been down. And I had the same beads on and the same "Hi ya, boys" style so that I could get laid.

Don't tell me I'm a star, man.

Above and opposite: Country blues singer, Austin, Texas, 1965
[PAT "SUNSHINE" NICHOLS/COURTESY OF RICHARD HUNDGEN]

you left me to face it alone

Mornings were always the worst for Janis, tired and sodden, gluing herself together on the spur of the moment for the trip to the airport. Some mornings she looked as if she'd been run over in her sleep. Like a moth brutally caught in a blinding light, she staggered out of her motel room into the glare of the early afternoon.

Pain seeped into her by day and evaporated at night—first thing in the morning, even the Southern Comfort tastes bitter. It was close to a chemical infection, and it bred in her a low grade despair that fell into her head like water tapping at the bottom of a well.

Even her fatalism, ultimately relaxing, and her personal store of wisdom could not brace her against the blows when they came. Comfort is made of compromises and Janis would have no part of its nasty cycle. A paralysis of Kozmical despair seemed to be at the center of her everyday life. She carried around with her the weight of this realization that finally crushed her with all the mysterious forms that despair gives rise to. She carried the Troubled Truth about like the goat carrying the mountain in a wry Sufi fable.

It is called the Troubled Truth for good reason, since it is only when you *know* that life becomes intolerable. As John Lennon said: "If you don't know, man, then there's no pain." Janis could see into her own murky depths with chilling perception, and if she saw that her personal happiness was illusory, it was not because she had not thought about it or tried to work it out as best she could. These insights, however, only seemed to compound the pain.

Alcohol and drugs became the obvious conspirators in her *causa sui* project, magical partners hired for a time (and at colossal expense) to put to sleep the overwhelming odds.

The worst of it was that it wasn't a personal problem at all, it was just that in her secret way she took responsibility for it. But the Great Saturday Night Swindle was simply a condition of the world, *that's* was what was so depressing.

A kind of incipient fatalism took hold in Janis, not exactly a cynical philosophy, just an inverted blessing to hold back the flood. Janis would have given a lot to be a little *more* cynical, to cut away some of the weight, to turn a bit of it loose: "Untie me, god of knots!"

Even her formidable myth, constructed like some opulent dream, could not quiet the gnawing evidence, and after a certain point there was no going back. At the worst of times, these constructions and facades only helped to make things seem more hopeless than they actually were, as if personal storms had torn holes in all her grandiose sets, leaving the punctured scrims to flap mockingly at her head as sudden gusts ripped through her.

"why should i be afraid since there's nothing here but me?"

Just say she was someone
So far from home
Whose life was so lonesome
She died all alone
Who dreamed pretty dreams
That never came true
Lord, why was she born
So black and blue

Kris Kristofferson,
"Epitaph (Black and Blue)"

Few people were closer to Janis than John Cooke. In answer to the somewhat heartless and melodramatic way her death was treated in *Rolling Stone*, he wrote: "There is not the slightest suspicion in my mind that her death might have

Ratner's New York, 1968 [ELLIOT LANDY]

been intentional. She didn't believe in cutting short a rocking good time, and that was what she was having."

Of course it *wasn't* suicide, but what was it? And does it matter anyway, now that Janis is no bigger than the spot of blood that day on her new silk pants that Richard DiLello showed me in the photograph he'd taken of her in front of one of her twelve-foot posters outside the Albert Hall? I remember how, at the time, that little decimal point stopped my circulation, dazed for congealed moments as I thought about that body that couldn't live quietly, just as it stopped again when I heard that that lethal point had stung her for the last time.

"Who asked you to work your life away just trying to entertain us?" wrote a girl from Boston in one of the many angry, rhetorical letters addressed to Janis after her death.

A lot of people found it difficult to believe that Janis's death, if it wasn't suicide, wasn't exactly an accident either, that Janis, too, had seen it coming. The disappointment you could see in Janis's eyes sometimes could make you cry. Not when she was whining or bitching in her plaintive croaky voice, but sometimes when everything just seemed to overwhelm her.

Was it just a form of romantic self-pity that made Janis, after Jimi's death, tell friends (among them her polar twin, Little Richard), "Goddammit, he beat me to it"?

The first time I heard anyone talk about the possibility of Janis's death was on the train trip across Canada. I was talking to someone in Delaney and Bonnie's band about following Janis around for a while and writing a book about her. "You'd better hurry up," he said. "She's not going to be around much longer." I was a little stunned, but I put it down to the kind of hip bravado popular at the time.

Anyway, it seemed such an unlikely possibility. What could possibly do Janis in? She seemed as solidly situated on the earth as Mount Rushmore. I could even imagine her as an old lady. Maybe not as Lillian Roxon saw her, in tweeds and a couple of strands of pearls, but I *could* see her as a grandmother rocking on a porch somewhere.

It never occurred to me that it might be Janis who would do herself in, although, if you thought about it, the equation was perfect—and lethal. Afterwards, it was only too obvious that there'd been a relentless internal struggle going on all along.

The Grateful Dead grew up with Janis on the streets of the Haight-Ashbury, played music with her, got stoned with her and (a privilege granted to few others) let her get them drunk. Janis died during "Cold Rain and Snow" in the Dead's set at Winterland. Jerry Garcia, with the affection of an old friend, looked her death stoically in the face.

"Like, everybody does it the way they do it. Death only matters to the person that's dying. The rest of us are going to live without that voice. For those of us for whom she was a person, we'll have to do without the person.

"Janis was a *real person*. She went through all the changes we did. She went on all the same trips. She was just like the rest of us—fucked up, strung out, in weird places. Back in the old days, the pre-success days, she was using all kinds of things, just like anybody.

"When she went out after something, she went out after it really hard, harder than most people ever think to do, ever conceive of doing.

"She was on a real hard path. She picked it, she chose it, it's OK. She was doing what she was doing as hard as she could, which is as much as any of us can do. She did what she had to do and closed her books. I don't know whether it's *the* thing to do, but it's what *she* had to do.

"It was the best possible time for her death. If you know any people who passed that point into decline, you know, getting messed up, old, senile, done in. But going up, it's like a skyrocket, and Janis was a skyrocket chick.

"She had a sense of all that, including the sense that if somebody was making a movie of it, it'd make a great movie. If you had a chance to write your life . . . I would describe that as a good score in life writing, with an appropriate ending."

God it gets so lonely
when the fire is in your veins
when all ya' got is one
last shot

to get it right again

From "Sheila" by Eric Andersen

Outside Albert Hall, London, 1968 [RICHARD DILELLO]

THE MECHANICS OF ECSTASY

Upon the planes of ritual, ecstacy and metaphysics, ascension is capable, among other things, of abolishing Time and Space and of "projecting" man into the mythical instant of the Creation of the World, whereby he is in some sense "born again," being rendered contemporary with the birth of the World . . . when existence and Time first became manifest . . . . The radical "cure" of the suffering of existence is attained by retracing one's footsteps in the sand of memory.

Mircea Eliade, *Myths, Dreams and Mysteries*

backstage louisville

ady Reporter: Do you drink before going on stage?

Janis: I never drink until right before I go on. If I drink three or four hours before I go on, an hour before I go on, plus while I'm on, I'm not gonna enjoy the show because I'm not gonna remember it. I decided a couple of weeks ago that the music sounded so good that I wanted to be there, man. People used to tell me, "Wow, you did this and that," and I'd say, "Wow, it sounds great. I wish I'd been there."

David: The band sounds great, really right there.

Janis: Honey, honey, I'm telling you, they're great, man. I'm so fuckin' proud of them. I'm just so jacked to work with them, every day I just kiss 'em and tell 'em I love 'em, man. It's better than it's ever been for me. They're right behind me. They *follow* me, do you notice? When I go down they go "bop," when I go up they go "bop, bop, bop." They're so great. Really big talent.

Lady Reporter: How did you find them?

Janis: Oh, here and there. Albert found some of them for me. Some of them met somebody else.

David: How come you changed from horns?

Janis: Volume. Too many people complained there was too much noise. I like having horns, man. I like having the punch that horns give you. But they're too much trouble on the road, too much noise, too much crowding on stage. It just didn't work out. I like working with horns because it really gives you that "pow!" I really need it, man. But then there's all those Tuesday mornings in the hotel, people not showing up when they're supposed to.

Lady Reporter: What do people say when you wear those clothes in hotels and restaurants?

Janis: Yeah, they're real rude to me. They treat me like someone they don't want in there, and they *don't* want me in there. But it depends on how hard they are. You can leave and say, "Fuck them, I don't have to take this," or you show your money, and they allow you to stay. Everybody who looks weird gets fucked over. I look pretty weird, but I do the best I can!

David: Why do you think people want to fight with people who look weird?

Janis: I guess it's that whole thing you hear about. Because they're scared. That's what they're trying to say; because they don't like you is why. But why they don't like you I don't know—whether it's a reasonable reason or whether it's hung-up prejudice reason. Maybe their son is dropping acid, or maybe they think you're trying to hold up the banks. Basically, it's because you're on a different trip from them.

David: I think they say, "I'm not allowed to look like that. How come they can get away with it?" Don't you think?

Janis: Maybe so. Maybe they just don't like your fuckin' ass.

Lady Reporter: Are you a pessimistic person?

Janis: Aaaaahhh . . . I used to think so. I was a real pessimist, a real cynical bitch. Then I read somewhere this definition that said, "A pessimist is never disappointed, and an optimist is constantly let down." So by that definition I'd be an optimist. But I consider myself rather cynical. They called me a fine-feathered bird last week. "Here comes the fine-feathered bird."

David: Who said that?

Janis: Oh, a friend of mine. One of my crazy friends.

Lady Reporter leaves. Janis asks me what do I think she'll write.

David: I know she's going to write something good.

Janis: You never can tell. . . . Sometimes they think they're gonna like you. And then you get out there and you really damage and offend their femininity. You know, "No chick is supposed to stand like *that*." I mean, crouching down in front of the guitar player goin' "uuuuhhhn!" You know, lettin' your tits shake around, and your hair's stringy, you have no makeup on, and sweat running down your face, you're coming up to the fuckin' microphone, man, and at one point their heads just go "click," and they go, "Oooh, no!" You get that a lot. It's really far out. When you're standing on stage you can't see the whole crowd. The trouble is the groovy crowd is usually in the back, because they can't afford the seats down front—the seats down front are the local rich people, the local doctors' sons and their country club dates. They're the ones that are just sitting there, man, with their knees just so. You know, only cross at your ankles, keep your panty girdle tight together, and you sit with your hands in your lap. And I'm up there singing, I'm going, "Cha-cha-boom-quack-quack," and I look out at the crowd and the front rows are goin'— these girls have these little pinched smiles and the expressions on their faces are of absolute *horror*. They've never seen anything like it, and they don't want to again, man. The chick's up there, shakin' it all and sayin', "How do you like that, boys?" and all the boys are goin', "Aaaaaaghhh!" The girls are going, "Oh, my God, she may be able to sing, but she doesn't have to act like that!" That's the way *I* was raised, man. I know exactly what's on those bitches' minds. They don't like me, man. But that's not most of them. I figure most of them who go to the trouble to buy a ticket to come to my shows are ready to rock.

David: A lot of chicks in the audience are really behind you.

Janis: Yeah, but that's the trouble—the lights, you can't see them.

David: A lot of 'em really identify with you.

At my concerts most of the chicks are looking for liberation. They think I'm gonna show 'em how to do it, how to get down But the ones right in the front are always the country club bitches. They always are. It's so *weird* playing to fourteen panty girdles. Very strange. That's the trouble on stage. You can't see. I used to get really uptight when they turned on the house lights because I thought it would cool the show. But I noticed, in the past year, it doesn't. You turn on the house lights and if you've got an audience that's a little timid, the minute they see everybody else standing up and getting goony, they say, "What the fuck!" and everybody just stands up and starts getting sweaty. I used to think, with the lights on, if they couldn't see me singularly and watch me turn them on, they wouldn't get turned on. But now I know if they can see each other get turned on, they're gonna get turned on all the more. The fact that I'm standing there looking small and human like I do when the lights are on don't matter one fuckin' bit. They're scared at a lot of shows. Then they stand up, clap, stomp—nobody can really see me cause the stage is dark—and the lights are on them and they go, "Right on!" Then I know I've succeeded.

I'm a strong believer in magic. I'd fly across the country to see Otis for ten minutes. I'd go to see Little Richard anywhere. I'd go see Tina anywhere. Because they *work*, they *happen*, they're *electric*, they're *exciting*, they sweat for you. Fuck, they're so great, man, I just love 'em.

David: Otis was great. When he came on stage he was like a flash of lightning.

Janis: It's what I tell the boys. It's what Sly's band is good at—what you're seeing up there is rhythm. You're going: "Chug-a-chug-a-chug-a-chug." Well, with those good groups you not only feel that rhythm, you not only hear it, but you see it. Like Otis, whenever he walked, he walked in time—"Got-to-get-my-got-to-chug-a-chug." Sly does it too—"Higher, higher." They *move*, they make the song visible. You feel like your whole brain is just 1-2-3-4 rhythm.

John Cooke (in a nasal delivery-boy tone): Western Union, ma'am. They're just starting an underground press in this town, and there's a young man here with long hair from the underground press who wants to talk to you.

Janis: Is he sexy?

John: Well, I don't know. I'm not a connoisseur of young men. There's some nice-looking little girls out there, but they're all jailbait. So what do I tell this guy? Tell him you don't ever want to see him?

Janis: Tell him I'll answer a few questions. I don't want to do an interview.

Hippie Reporter: What do you expect the concert to come off like tonight?

Janis: I think it's gonna be double dynamite, man. I'm planning on having a good time.

Hippie Reporter: There's a Southern Comfort and Ripple party tonight in your honor.

Janis: Whooooo!

Hippie Reporter: What do you think of Louisville now that you've seen it?

Janis: I haven't seen it. I've been from the airport to the hotel, and the hotel to the bar, and the bar to the room and the room to here.

Hippie Reporter: How long have you been on the road now?

Janis: This tour? Not long. I don't look so good, man. I look tired. I don't mind if I'm on stage. You know, it's funny. Like most girls, I'm always really self-conscious about do I look fat, if my legs are short, if I'm weird shaped, but when

117

JIM MARSHALL

I go on stage, man, it never even occurs to me. I think I look beautiful.

Hippie Reporter: Are you back with Big Brother?
Janis: Oh, no!

Hippie Reporter leaves a few minutes later.

David: You've got to be kind to your own people, you know.
Janis: I'm not being kind?
David: Yeah, you are. You're cool.
Janis: He was scared. I could have been nicer. I should have been nicer, right? What am I supposed to do?
David: Everyone is nervous when they come to see you, you know, because you're such a star.
Janis: I can't relate to that, I can't relate to that. If they know anything about *anything*, they know I'm not a star. They know I'm a middle-aged chick with a drinking problem, man, and a loud voice, and other things, too. But, you know, fuck, there ain't nothing special about that.
David: What you do on stage is a complete mystery.
Janis: I don't *get* it, and I don't believe it. I just can't get it, conceptually.
David: Even Mick doesn't get up on stage and get into the music like that. That's fantastic! You have to be right there to do that. He takes two or three numbers to warm up; the first time he's self-conscious and putting himself on. But when you do it, it's incredible.
Janis: Well, I can't relate to that. False modesty, man.
David: Well, let's put it down to that.
Janis: Fuck you.
David: Also, people are intimidated by you because you're such a large figure.
Janis: I lost a lot of weight.
David: I mean symbolically.
Janis: I'm just fucking with you, man.

David: Did he leave his notes here? You see how nervous he was?

Janis: I know he was nervous. But what am I supposed to do? Turn around and say, "I'm a person!"?

David: It's hard. But, anyway, he went away thinking how great you are, because that's what he came here thinking.

Janis: Why do they come to see me—I don't know what they think I know.

David: They just want to see you. You're a star.

Janis: Pshaw! No, I don't think I'm a star. I'll never be a star like Jimi Hendrix or Bob Dylan. I figured out why—cause I tell the truth. If they want to know who I am, they ask me and I'll tell them.

Reviewing *Pearl* in *Rolling Stone*, Jack Shadoian wrote:

> Her last album can't simply be an occasion for evaluation. The fact that there will be no more studio albums inevitably outweighs the issue of how good or how bad the record might be. Besides, Janis was a heavy, and had incredible presence whether at the top or bottom of her form. She was a remarkable, if erratic, singer, and she proved it, live and on record. Anyone who exhibits qualities of greatness earns certain privileges—not critical immunity so much as the right to be forever removed from inconsequentiality: all their work, flawed or not, is worth experiencing. Would you rather listen to bad Monk or good Ramsey Lewis? Or, if Monk could ever be called bad, could Lewis ever be called good? In certain instances, "good" and "bad" can be pretty useless terms. It's Janis, or it's Monk, and you listen, and you care, because you know that whatever is going down is genuine and may contain a revelation, and a possibility that may be written off in the case of lesser artists.

Unlike the blues singers whom she admired and emulated, Janis was not a classic blues singer. To some she took the blues farther than Bessie Smith and Billie Holiday had ever gone, and to others she contaminated a classic form with wretched excesses. But her blues were of another order altogether—one which precludes comparisons. This is perhaps why so much articulate (and inarticulate fury) was generated by pointless comparisons.

Few of the numinous singers of the sixties had what might be called a "good" voices. Vocal polishing was more an element of the fifties and those sixties groups who did achieve it—the Beach Boys, the Four Seasons, the Mamas and the Papas—don't mesh easily with mainstream sixties folk heroes from Dylan to the Stones. It's almost as if that articulation of harmony and manicured vocal inflection was too produced, its surface too smooth to hook onto.

The originators of rock 'n' roll had little regard for vocal purity: Chuck Berry, Bo Diddley, Howlin' Wolf, Jerry Lee, and Little Richard. All dirty, "gutsy" singers.

You could almost say that this unpolished quality of rock is its most tangible feature. As Janis, with typical subjective precision, put it: "I don't worry about whether it's musical, but did it get off?"

on the knees of the heart

Natives widely believe that the essence of a person, song, object resides within, not on the surface, not in outward appearances . . . insisting that reality isn't in them but in the laws that govern bodies; or in the sense that Picasso, to show a total being, takes us right inside.

From this comes the belief that although the world consists of bodies, each contains within itself an essence, power, vital energy, which under certain conditions is given out, illuminating, changing whatever it touches. When such energy meets forces radiating from another being, something new may be created. Similarly, forces from other beings may penetrate one, enter one, change one. One may "drink in" another. Be possessed by another. Become *inspired.*

Edmund Carpenter,
They Became What They Beheld

No matter how dissipated-looking Janis got, on stage she always looked like the unicellular child: reckless, extreme, indulgent, and radiant. Janis stretched each moment to its absolute limit.

In this projection there is an almost superhuman effort involved, because the audience will only believe the dream, and thereby liberate within themselves the magic freedom of dreams, if it is thrust upon them violently.

Janis's talent for dealing in collective identities made such rushes all the more plausible. *Okay, Kansas, you and I are going to come to grips* Or what she said to a country deejay who had just stolen a kiss, "Honey, you just took on Port Arthur!" On stage this habit of sweeping all these individual specks of pulverized appearances into a momentary Leviathan was more concrete. With her mesmerizing intensity she welded together all the threads, scales and fragments of our collective person, as if she were piecing Humpty Dumpty back together again.

Through music's anarchic power to both disassociate and, ultimately, to integrate, Janis let us know that only *all* of us can see it. Too vast to guess by parts; too enclosed within us for us to recognize.

"Back in Port Arthur, I'd heard some Leadbelly records, and, well, if the blues syndrome is true, I guess it's true about me. So I began listening to blues and folk music. I bought Bessie Smith records, and Odetta and Billie Holiday . . . ," says Janis, visiting herself.

Funky as Janis was, she was closer in style to Bessie Smith than to raunchier blues singers like Ma Rainey. Rainey gravitated towards rough jazz band or solo guitar accompanists like Tampa Red, while Bessie preferred to be backed by a professional orchestra like Fletcher Henderson's. Bessie's bows and tassels were in sharp contrast to Ma's necklace of twenty-dollar gold pieces and the pearls slung around her neck like tiny hard sacks of flour.

There was something wistful about Bessie, and that was also in Janis. Bessie, like Janis, was more theatrical than the earthy country blues singers they emulated. Both enjoyed the delicious artificiality of the theater, where stars arrive on stage from a different dimension—"the wings."

"Performers aren't people," says the thief in *The Children of Paradise*, "they're everybody at the same time."

ШШШ western union **Telegram**

```
LD68 BG PDF  LOUISVILLE KY 702P JUN 12
JANICE JOPLIN DLY .75
   CARE BOX OFFICE STATE FAIR AND EXPOSITION CENTER
   FREEDOM HALL LVILLE
WELCOME WE INVITE YOU TO A SOUTHERN COMFORT AND RIPPLE
PARTY TONIGHT AFTER YOUR PERFORMANCE AT THE FREE PRESS
OFFICE LOVE.
      THE FREE PRESS STAFF 1438 SOUTH FIRST FREE UNION OF
      COLLECTIVE KARMA AND THE YIP YIP WATERMELON TRIBE
                         707P
```

"i'm gonna use it till the day i die"

"Even the articulate or brutal sounds of the globe," De Quincey wrote in his *Autobiography*, "must all be so many languages and ciphers that somewhere have their corresponding keys—have their own grammar and syntax; and thus the least things in the universe must be secret mirrors to the greatest."

Freedom Hall, where the concert took place, is a monster indoor stadium designed for wrestling matches and basketball games, the kind of place that looks empty even when it's full to capacity. With an audience of about 4,000, it looked pretty sad. To make matters worse, the crowd, mostly younger kids in neat hippy/mod clothes, did not *look* like Janis's crowd.

Janis took a peek between the curtains before going on and realized it is not exactly Angel's Night at the Avalon Ballroom.

It took a while for the audience to get into it, but Janis was having *her* party, and she was just waiting for them to come over.

"Some dance hall you got here," Janis said hand-on-hip, Bette Davis style. "You know, sometimes we go into a place and take a quick look at the hall, a quick look at the dressing rooms, and a quick look at the audience, and we say, 'Well, if we're going to have a party here, we're just going to have to do it ourselves . . . . ' "

"Try Just a Little Bit Harder," a girl shouted out as a request, and Janis yelled back, "I beg your pardon. I'm doing *my* part, honey."

If things started slowly, the concert ended in a near-riot, and the rent-a-cops in their Mountie hats, not sure whether they were at a concert or a demonstration, began driving back the kids rushing the stage, leading with their clubs and flashlights. Janis meanwhile was ecstatic.

"I permit them to dance," she yelled to a burly sergeant-at-arms, "in fact, I demand it!" And the rent-a-cop marched up and down, scowling and fuming and shaking his fist at Janis in a gesture of revenge, and for a minute it looked like one of those movies where the good-hearted rainmaker gets run out of town. But, in fact, everybody had a good time except the rent-a-cops, who couldn't figure out what role to play and ended up overacting.

It all broke loose when Janis launched into "Try," with her jive about, "Honey, if you've had your eye on a piece of talent and that chick down the road has been getting all the action, then you know what you gotta do. . . . " And *wham!* the drum kicks into the song and Janis lays on her message: "Try just a little bit harder."

As she got into it, she jumped off the stage, and a kid in the front row started shaking it down with her. That was all that was needed. Everybody got out of, onto, or over their chairs and stayed dancing, shouting and clapping.

From there things just kept grinding on, with "Summertime," "Kozmic Blues" and "Move Over." By the time she got into her last number, "Piece of My Heart," security had all the house lights turned on in the hope that it would cool everybody out, but it had just the opposite effect. The kids saw that *everybody* was standing, dancing up and down and screaming and it just made them wilder. Eventually the whole audience swarmed up to the stage like a hive of bees.

In this conservative Southern town, it was as if Janis had flashed a vision of the Garden of Eden at them. And they didn't want it to end.

They were grateful to Janis for taking them away from where they were and putting their heads somewhere else and they showed it. Janis was exhausted but excited; the rain dance had worked. As Janis and the band left the stage in the eternal rock pantomime of unplugging guitars, the crowd howled for more.

David Dalton, *"Janis Joplin's Full Tilt Boogie Ride,"*
Rolling Stone, August 6, 1970

Janis takes another sip of Southern Comfort and hits the encore. The first doomy sounds of "Ball and Chain" on the guitar always told of the end with the inevitability of a twelve bar blues, and as Janis wails into those last impossible notes, we know that we are outside musical terms.

Whirring horrors and wards of sorrow, all attended and nursed by fierce, volatile "head" notes, rush from every corner

of the universe to gather up everything that is unresolved in Janis's life. All the monstrous sounds, painful and pathetic, human and sub-human, known and imagined, bear witness to the bottomless sadness that inhabited her.

Noises full of real terror: the whining of dogs, the croaking of drains, shrieks of scraping metal—all possess Janis's body from moment to moment, tossing her mercilessly.

Two voices struggle for possession in a cracked harmony, while an army of "I's" pierce the air. Words pile up in stuttering clumps of confusion.

> *Aaah want* someone to tell me,
> got to tell me—
> whyiiiiiiiiiiii!
> Just because I got to want your luuuuv . . .
> Honeh, jus because I need, need, need your love
> I said, honey, I don't understand.
> B-b-b-b-b-but, honeh, I wanna chance to trrry
> i-i-i-i-i-i-i-i-i-i-i-i-i-i-i-I-I-I-I-I!
> try, try, try, try, tri-i-i-i-i-!-huh-huh-huh-huh-i-i!

Little Richard called "the voices" with which Janis, like the holy roller tentshow queen, pursued her demons, "a sign of her possession by the Holy Spirit which she brought with her out of the South." We may not use precisely these terms, but we nevertheless believe that the waywardness and compulsiveness of Janis's voices come from violent forces and secret causes that forced her soul into their own shape.

As if awakened by her own voice in a dream, Janis comes out of her trance and blithely walks into a rap: "I don't understand, how come . . . you're *gone*, man. I don't understand why half the world is still cryin' . . . when the other half of the world is still cryin', too, man. I can't get it either. I mean, if you got a cat for one day, man . . . and say, maybe you want a cat for 365 days . . . . You ain't got him for 365 days. You got him for one day. Well, I tell you, that one day, man, had better be your life. Because you can say . . . oh, man, you can cry about the other 364. But you're gonna lose that one day, man, and that's all you got. You gotta call that love, man. That's what it is, man. If you got it today, you don't want it tomorrow, man. Cause you don't need it. Cause, as a matter of fact, tomorrow never happens, man. It's all the same fuckin' day."

The Big Open Notes take off on their journey through space, flying past at the speed of light. Their only reference point is Janis. We are invited to follow their dizzying, painful flight or remain pinned to our fixed states. Their capsule of sound is constantly shifting, but the careening Notes, concerned only with where they're going, at first forget what they're travelling in, although its outline is as familiar to them as a Terraplane or an old Plymouth.

"If you keep this up, we're going to have an accident," says a clanging E chord from "After You've Gone." Suddenly they realize that what is propelling them recklessly forward is more the *idea* of a car, and that all the notes jiggling and dancing around them are just as much the idea of a highway, and as they feel themselves, a little late, slamming on the brakes, they know they have crashed blissfully through to the other side of Everything:

> *hah-hah-hah-hah-huhn-hhaaahaaaahhhaaahaaaah*
> *hold on like it's the last moment of your life, because some day*
> *a weight's gonna come on your shoulders, babeh*
> *and it's gonna feel just like a ball . . .*
> *anuhnananananuhn-hauhnhahahuhn*
> *nananuhnananuhn-ni-i-i-i-i-i-uuuhn*
> *chayayayayayayayayayayn!*

bar talk

When it came to bars Janis was absolutely fearless; she would walk in anywhere. She'd plunk herself down at the bar, heel hooked around the rail and elbow crooked in the padded ledge, as if to keep herself from drifting away.

In spite of the alcoholic fraternity of such places, Janis was always alert, an acolyte in the service of W. C. Field's devotional equation: "When you woo a wet goddess, there's no use falling at her feet." She would become repetitious and ornery but rarely foggy or boring. It was amazing, therefore, how often she tolerated the most incredibly maudlin, obnoxious drinking partners.

I came down one morning to find Janis settled into the motel bar as if it were a fat, familiar armchair. To Janis's right a black entertainer is relating an interminable epic. His story cranks on and on, bristling with details and turning endlessly on itself. To her left a contentious Southern gentleman alternates between come-ons and local history.

Reviews of the concert are scattered all over the table. The local papers are ecstatic. The *Louisville Times* calls it a "love feast." The piece by the Lady Reporter, titled "Rock Queen Blasts Off Like an Apollo Rocket," launches into some pyrotechnic journalism:

> Like an Apollo rocket blasting off—that's the power of Janis Joplin's voice. Howling, screeching, and penetrating the air with such brilliance and force, you believe for a moment she could fill the Grand Canyon with sound.

That was amazing last night.

And, dig it, that was only our fifth gig. One, two, three, four, five. We're only just now getting our shit together. The band, for instance, had never seen me jump off the stage before. I do all kinds of stuff like that. They've never seen me come on stage and say "Pow! come on, stand up! dance!" right to those boys in the front row, and gettin' those country club boys going, "Aaaaghhh, aaaaaghhh!" Wooooooooooh!

That guy got up and really did it. It was beautiful.

Yeah! He grabbed my tits. That's the first thing he did. Got somethin' goin'. Once you jump on the floor and start dancin' with them, unless they're *sound asleep*, that usually gets 'em up. There's somethin' really strange I've noticed, there's some kind of artificial barrier built into their minds between stage and us—*that's* the stage, *that's* the show. It's like an invisible wall between stage and audience. Once you break that barrier, and you jump down and walk out and touch 'em, and say, "I'll dance with you, man, I'll get sweaty with you. Come on, I'm with *you*, man . . . ." In fact, *I* just happen to be standing on stage. Once they feel that barrier is down, that they're there with you it just rocks right on out, man. It's fun, it's fun. I used to get such a rush from that *contact*, man, and, as a matter of fact I still do. You *gotta* get yourself off first for them to get into it. You gotta love it cause that's the only reason to be doin' it.

I got a beautiful home, and here I am sittin' in Louisville, Kentucky, it's raining, I'm in the bar, it's noon, I'm being treated rudely by four people out of five.

Really, Janis?

Listen, until I got the reviews in here, honey. . . .

You mean you weren't too popular in here?

Not *exactly* . . . . How're you doin', honey? Think we're gonna make it this time around?

The band is great and I'm having a good time . . . .

Bein' on stage, man, rockin' out, like everything else is like lookin' at yourself in the mirror. That's the one thing I've learned about being on the road; that that music and that hour you get on stage is *all*. The rest of it is fucked up. People tryin' to get something out of you, tryin' to talk to you. Try to sleep, you can't sleep, nothin' on the tube. At two the bars are closed. It's just *uuuuuugghh*! It ain't really a rockin' good

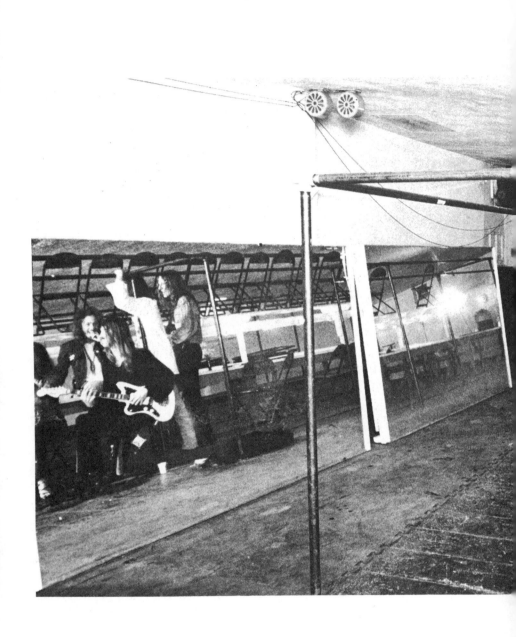

Backstage, Winterland, 1968

time. The rockin' good times you create, you bring the bottle yourself and go to someone else's room and say, "Let's rock."

The road is just a hassle, the only thing you got out of it that's groovy is playin'. Any musician that I see that's workin', especially those six-days-a-week cats, they're only *doing it* cause they love music. There's *no other reason*. No money is worth that . . . that grief, man. I have a beautiful home; I could be playing with my dogs and havin' my friends come over and visit me. But I'd rather be here with a hangover—trying to get myself together to go to a movie to cure absolute abject boredom in Louisville, Kentucky.

What do you think about what the Louisville *review said about Big Brother?*

It's a very sad thing. I love those guys more than anybody else in the whole world, they know that. But if I had any serious ideas of myself as a musician, I had to leave. Getting off, real *feeling*, that's the whole thing of music for me. But by the end, we were shucking. We worked four, six nights a week for two years, doing the same tunes, and we'd put everything into them we could. We just used each other up.

I always thought Big Brother was a really great band for you.

Maybe it was, man, and maybe I'll never find another one as good, but at the time. . . . Here's the way I see the problem. Peter Albin thinks I'm wrong. He sees it another way. Ego problems or whatever. I loved them, I still love them more than I love anyone else, and I'll never be as close to anyone in the world. James and Sam, those are the two men in my life, y'know?

But there was all kinds of problems—like success came early. We never had a chance to rehearse any more, and when we did rehearse we never got any new material. We were on the road, we hit New York once, and bang! we were a big smash. Toured, toured, toured, toured, toured, a three week rest in California and, bang! hit the road again, no rehearsing. We're still doing "Combination of the Two," "Ball and Chain," "Combination of the Two," "Ball and Chain." We've bin doin' it for a year now. We were startin' on the second year, "Combination of the Two," "Ball and Chain". . . .

As far as I'm concerned what drove me crazy was that I couldn't dredge up any sincerity in the music anymore. I mean, it wasn't anybody's fault. It's maybe the fault that we got too much work. Maybe it was that everybody got too lazy, y'know? Which I think definitely is true. They thought, "why work, man, they like it." We weren't doin' anything *new* and I kept singin' the same old songs every night. Finally I said to myself, listen, man, you consider yourself a singer, but you're nothin' but an actor. I wanted to do some new shit. I had new ideas, maybe not concrete ones—like I couldn't walk out and do the arrangements—but I had a feeling of the way I wanted it to move. I wasn't doing anything but standing still and being a success.

So I quit. Lots of people think it was a mistake and it well may have been a mistake. Those guys in Big Brother certainly loved me more than anybody else ever will. And that showed on the stage. But we were *enacting* it up there, man, we weren't lovin' each other. We knew when the lights went on it was a show.

See, maybe in a few years I'll have a different head, maybe I'll have developed that professional distance that says if it succeeds, it's a success, y'know? But at that time. . . . and I still am, I'm a beat, I started out in the world to be a beatnik, I wanted to do what felt right to me. I didn't want to be an executive or a teacher just because I could've. I didn't want to be something just to make money. I wanted to be something because it felt right to me. When it ceases to *feel* right, I think you oughta change, even if you are making a lot of money.

I was very shaky at the beginning, everybody thought I was gonna go under. But I refused to. That's what it pretty much boiled down to. An article coming out in *Playboy* next week says I was a failure. Everyone says Janis lost it when she quit Big Brother. But I just wouldn't quit, man.

Rolling Stone said I was a failure. It's a real old article, way, way last year, when the San Francisco audience deserted me when I came out with my new group. They just turned their backs on me.

Okay, we *weren't* as good as Santana. We'd only fuckin' been together *two months*. It will take a long while, I'm not a pro. I've only been with, y'know, a bunch of friends, heretofore. All of a sudden I'm faced with a pro group, trying to figure out material, arrange it, turn it into a product, which took me a while to get the feeling right. I think we're just now getting the feeling right. I want to learn how to *stretch* out a little bit; now it's still too crowded with Janis. But as soon as the guys get a little more confidence, I think it'll just flow like it's supposed to. I wasn't quittin', man, but right then, at the beginning, nobody put a dime on my chances, 'cept me. I ain't quittin', man. I won't quit for *nobody*.

They'll have to throw me out if they want me to get out.

"there must be more to love than this"

There is no show tonight, and the evening gapes ahead of us. There's a fantastic country & western show at the civic center: George Jones (from Beaumont, next door to Janis's hometown of Port Arthur), Tammy Wynette, and Jerry Lee Lewis. A moment's hesitation. Janis voices the paranoia: "You know what it's gonna be, dontcha? Ten thousand fuckin' shitkickers goin' goony."

Janis, Clark Pierson and I resolve to go anyway, but late. Tammy Wynette is just about Janis's least favorite singer, so we miss the first half. To add to the surrealism of Janis in hillbilly heaven, the auditorium is right next door to some kind of penitentiary. Sloping up from backstage is a ramp with two guards cradling shotguns in their arms and patrolling a couple of open gratings.

Janis's credentials are not immediately recognized at the stage door. "Janis Joplin's the name," she says pointedly to the keeper of the gate. "I'm a singer—you *might* recognize my name." Eventually the emcee, a hearty Texan in a white ten-gallon hat, ushers us in.

The scene inside is hard to believe. The crowd is close to 20,000 and this initially brings Janis down. "How come they didn't come see me 'n' then they come here to listen to all that old music?" she asks, a little naively. Every woman here looks like Tammy Wynette or Dolly Parton in that sculptured, glossy helmet-like hairdo which always looks tarty to urban eyes. They're wearing little peek-a-boo dresses that have a kind of rural innocence, as if they were still doing the Tennessee Waltz, and their dates, sleek as otters, slink back in their seats in Arnold Palmer golf sweaters and white Vent-Aire loafers.

We are allowed to stand behind the ramps. A conciliatory usher waves us back with Southern gentility. Janis manages to sneak by just the same. As chance would have it, the concert manager is the very same sergeant-at-arms who was in charge of keeping order at Janis's concert. He's on home ground now and he's about to take full advantage of it. "Listen," he says threatening in a bloated fury, "I hay-ud enough of yew last ni-ut. Yew get the hail owt of ma sight!"

Meanwhile on stage Jerry Lee is getting into his big hit, "The Beer That Made Milwaukee Famous (Has Made a Loser Out of Me)." His slightest gesture sends the crowd into seething paroxysms. "You should be thanking your lucky stars they're not cannibals," Clark Pierson says grimly.

The taunting of the sergeant-at-arms eventually becomes too much for Janis and she crashes after him with the wobbling fury of a derailed train. "Tell me where to go, asshole, and I'll go. Just LEAVE ME THE FUCK ALONE. Go on, you *jerk-off*, you're the motherfucker that stopped my show." He completely ignores her, and just as he is turning away to attend to something at the other end of the auditorium, Janis pulls out an empty bourbon bottle that she is about to crack him with. It takes the combined strength of Clark and me to pull her off.

Janis's attention soon turns to more immediate things. She's developed an almost frightening attraction for Jerry Lee's bass player, a 17-year-old hillbilly from Texas with long blond hair sleeked back like yellow sealskin.

"I must have that bow-ah," Janis says with contagious country inflection. "He is *one* bee-yute-ee-full boy."

By this time Jerry Lee is getting into his finale, snapping at the keys like a combine harvester. He kicks over his piano stool with contrived fury, but the gesture is so brutal that it stops you for a moment. The crowd is moaning and screaming. The waving of his suggestive pinky—"Wiggle it around a little bit"—is the equivalent of Moses parting the Dead Sea with his staff.

We go backstage with the emcee. Janis gets a better look at the bass player. And at close quarters, she thinks he looks better than ever. Janis is pointing and making signs to him while he's on stage, and he just stares back in complete incomprehension.

"Is that your band out there?" Janis asks the emcee dumbly.

"No, ma'am, that's the band that travels with Jerry Lee."

"Do you happen to know the bass player in the group?" Janis asks innocently. "I mean, would you introduce me to him when the group comes off stage?"

"I'd be happy to, Jane-is," he says civilly, not realizing what's coming next.

"Can't wait to get my hands on that *gorgeous*-looking boy," Janis says.

"For you?" the emcee asks incredulously. "God, Jane-is, fer shame. Why, he wouldn't even know what to do with you."

"What he doesn't know how to do, honey," Janis says with a Mae West inflection, "I'll be glad to show him."

By this time Janis is hopping up and down on stage shouting, "Play it, daddy, play it. Know something, man, that group is as tight as rope."

As the bass player comes off stage Janis grabs him. He's a little stunned by Janis's squeaky, "Waaal . . . hello there," and the ferocious arm lock she's got him in. Still a little spaced from the performance, he thinks maybe this is a not-too-distant relative or just an especially ardent fan. But his eyes shift visibly into reverse as the situation comes bogglingly into focus. Janis's intentions are about as well concealed as Sylvester's for Tweety Pie.

"You're not climbing on a bus going somewhere tonight, are you, honey?"

"Well, actually, yes ma'am, I guess I am."

"No, you're not, man. They told me you're not climbing on a bus. They told me you were all going to a party tonight, man," Janis says, confronting him like an irate mother.

"I guess I didn't know about any of that," he says, shifting his weight nervously.

But Janis is not about to let any of this country boy coyness get in the way of a good time.

"I thought we'd go back to the dressing room and get it on," Janis insists, but the kid is in a serious state of shock—lockjaw is setting in—and he slinks apologetically down the hall.

"What's the matter? Don't you like *sex*?" Janis shouts after him.

"Well, yeah . . . ," he says, fumbling for a doorknob. After he's gone, Janis asks rhetorically why none of the men she digs dig *her*. Clark philosophically offers an explanation: "Well, Janis, it could be your 'glad to meet you I'm yours' attitude."

"breathless . . . ah"

Linda Gail Lewis takes us back to see her brother. His dressing room has the smoky, sweaty aura of a locker room with the guys sitting around chewing the fat. Janis belongs here about as much as Queen Victoria would in Medicine Hat. "Hi ya, boys!" she hollers, tinkling into the room. "Hey, man, I saw a movie of you yesterday, the Toronto Festival. You were really cookin'!"

Jerry Lee is sitting with no shirt on astride a bench, surrounded by local deejays, buddies, and members of his group, mostly older Southern gentlemen who all wear weathered, hard-bitten, Wild Turkey faces cured on a diet of Jimmy Rodgers and mustard greens.

"It would be really better for your voice if you wrapped a towel around your throat," Janis says solicitously.

"Don't bother *me* none," Jerry Lee says testily.

"Would you like a *drink?*" Janis asks.

"I could go for a good strong one," Jerry Lee says.

"There ain't stronger than what I got, man. Southern Comfort."

"Yeah? I reckon that stuff is about 100 proof," Jerry Lee replies edgily.

"I do the best I can, what do you think I drink it for, boredom?"

Janis realizes that this isn't exactly her scene, but she digs it anyway. Janis is not exactly Jerry Lee's scene, either. He just doesn't know what to do with her, and he sure isn't going to compete. He's too subtle and sardonic for that. He sort of tailgates along as Janis boomerangs around the room. He looks at her searchingly, a sarcastic tilt to his head, as if she were a ballsy materialization of Yma Sumac.

"On a record of yours you've got a song by a silver-tongued devil by the name of Kris Kristofferson don'tcha?" Janis asks, awkwardly trying to start a conversation.

"That boy can sure drink wine, I can tell you."

"Not only wine, man. That cat can outdrink me in tequila, and I thought I could cover that on anyone. He was at my house three weeks. Couldn't leave."

"Him and . . . *Silverstein* . . . Didn't he write 'Once More With Feeling'?" Jerry Lee asks.

"Right, man, he kept playing that every morning soon as he got up," Janis cackles.

Jerry Lee can be very ornery. He isn't your typical country bumpkin, not by half a yard. No sir, this boy is *sharp*. You just have to hear the way he sings "She Only Woke Me Up To Say Goodbye" to know what brand of goods Jerry Lee has in his store.

Jerry Lee: "He wrote a real good song that I was gonna record one time, number one song it would've been. Anyway, I was drivin' and I heard this show on the radio, you know, one of those talk, interview type programs. And all he could talk about was Johnny Cash, Johnny Cash, Johnny Cash. When I got back I sent him this letter, said 'Why don't you send it to Johnny Reb?'

"How was your concert last night?" Jerry Lee adds, trying to get off this particular turnpike.

"We had a bony-fide, all-in, full-tilt freak-out, and then they tried to stop it."

"Was it a *riot?*" Jerry Lee asks sardonically.

"No, man, they just wanted to dance. Hey, it was at the Freedom Hall! Get it? They were beatin' my people on the head, man, and I just said 'out!' "

"Things *can* get out of hand," says Jerry Lee, palming it off.

"There ain't no such thing as outta hand, man. If the cops would leave them alone, there wouldn't be any trouble in the first place."

"Maybe they get wild because of you, Janis," Linda Gail suggests.

"Can't help it, man. Been this way for ten years. My mother threw me out of the house when I was 14."

combination of the two

> The exceptions, naturally, have a very unhappy childhood and youth; for to be essentially reflective at an age which is naturally immediate, is the depths of melancholy. But they are rewarded; for most people do not succeed in becoming spirit, and all the fortunate years of their immediateness are, where spirit is concerned, a loss, and therefore they never attain to spirit. But the unhappy childhood and youth of the exception is transfigured into spirit.
>
> Kierkegaard, *Journals, 1848*

Janis was born on January 19, 1943, under the sign of Capricorn. She was only mildly attached to the paraphernalia of astrology and psychedelia, although she did recognize in herself the afflictions of that sign—intense introspection and the tendency to go from the heights of ecstacy to the depths of depression. The goat on the peak, the fish in the deep.

She lived the pain of paradox, and if she had been named for the two-faced god of this month, Janus, god of gates and transitions, one face toward the past, the other toward the future, the choice could hardly have been more appropriate.

Janis's publicist, Myra Friedman, saw an almost total split between Janis's personal aspirations and the image by which she was best known: "The image she sometimes cultivated and sometimes had forced on her, that of the 'get it while you can girl,' was not accurate.

"I think Janis knew that wasn't really where she was at. Maybe a part of her believed that, but I think the most honest part of her didn't. She wasn't a conservative girl—that's ridiculous—but she had a lot of needs that were just like everyone else's. She was accepting of a lot of different kinds of people."

Sam Gordon, who ran Janis's music publishing company, told me of a conversation he'd had with Janis shortly before her death. "We were rapping about what we wanted from life, and I said I wished I was on the road again instead of in my comfortable suburban life I've been living for some time now.

"'I'll take a splitlevel bungalow with two kids any day,' she said. I asked if that was what she really wanted and she said, 'Yeah, that's what I really want.'"

This lesion of identity threatened to undermine everything Janis did. Perhaps this is the enigma presented to everyone who tries to scale the heights The wall of Paradise, which conceals God from man, is said to be constituted of a coincidence of opposites, its gate guarded by "the highest spirit of reason, who bars the way until he has been overcome," Nicholas of Cusa wrote in *De Visione Dei*. Pairs of opposites, which seem to have been more profuse in Janis than in most, are the rocks that crush the traveler, but through which the aspirant must pass.

Within Janis there raged continual conflict. She was the sensual child, straining at the leash, filled with poignant fears and delights, yearning for impossibly romantic meetings, night sounds and the perfume of wild flowers. But this child lived in fear of her *wraith*, a double-walker of ominous suggestion; the doubting, nagging parent, present at every wish. Caught between these forces, Janis crouched at the Hippocampal gate with only two defenses, smack and time.

In "Try", Janis sang, "If it's a dream, I don't want nobody to wake me." But only in dreams are such opposing contradictions as plagued Janis resolved. To lean too heavily on their fragile fabric is to impose the machinery of fantasy on unyielding matter. Fitzgerald had seen in Zelda this same fatal flaw, believing in the impossible and then attempting to set it in motion. "Her dominant idea and goal is freedom without responsibility, which is like gold without metal, spring without winter, youth without age, one of those maddening coo-coo mirages." *(The Crack-Up)*

So I said, "Hon, I want the sunshine
Yeah, take the stars out of the night.
Janis Joplin, *"Turtle Blues"*

"I was a sensitive child," Janis recalled. "I had a lot of hurts and confusions. You know, it's hard when you're a kid to be different. You're full of things, and you don't know what it's about."

In one way or another, anyone who was ever moved by her music or mesmerized by her galactic stage presence has experienced some of that pain. Her songs were just what she did with her sadnesses.

Janis's lost childhood and her limitless sadness precipitated in her a hidden inwardness and a personal life detached from all roots. It was an effect that in other, more religious times would have been called simply "spirit."

If Janis contributed anything to our culture, our freedoms even, it was this image of the gigantic child, absorbed in play, willing to let go the monster of self if it would let *her* go.

"my daddy stood all the way and cried"

There must have come a point when Janis came face to face with her constellated demons. One night, when no distractions filled the void, their breath must have impregnated her, just as God is said to have put the stars in the firmament, "all the host of them by the breath of His mouth." And like the insidious water grandfather of Russian folktales, with his spectral talent for coaxing into his toils unhappy young women who like to dance on moonlit nights, the demon must have seduced her in the sweet darkness.

Her parents could tell. And they were distressed and hurt to find that despite all their precautions their child had been infested with incubi. Her mother's rage was not even contained by Janis's death; she could never accept what Janis had "made of herself."

Janis grew up during the fifties, the adolescence of a new America, violent, pimply, naive, and stoked with inexpressible desires and energies that it did not know what to do with. This ambivalent time (half angry, half complacent) was a last, lingering moment of innocence before James Dean smashed through the windshield of America's past and brought on the perpetual teen dream. Janis was a capsule of all that undetonated energy forced in on itself, as if the decade had condensed in her, Little Queenie jumping up on stage and kissing the future.

Janis created her own style. It was her *hair.* "Positively triangular in its electricity," Lillian Roxon described it, and with compassionate insight caught Janis's truth beautifully: "I read with some sorrow, in *Time* magazine, I think it was, that someone said that before it all happened, the success and everything, Janis was a pig. But beauty had a way of flowing out again, so I guess there were as many times when she looked truly homely as there were times when she looked beautiful. And that went for a lot of her sisters. I think she taught America that beauty didn't *have* to be a constant, it could ebb and flow and surprise you by being there one minute and not the next."

Hair, the sexually loaded seed pod flowering from the roots of the head. The emergence of hair as a presence expresses the almost intangibly archaic idea, "that the head contains a different factor, the procreative life, soul or spirit that survives after death, and the seeds of a new life," as Onians said in *Origins of European Consciousness.*

Jimi Hendrix, in his own intuitive way, had made the connection. "Fuzzy hair is radiant. My hair is electric, man, it picks up *all* the vibrations."

With Bluebirds [DOROTHY JOPLIN. COURTESY OF JOPLIN FAMILY/RICHARD HUNDGEN]

Family album photo [COURTESY OF JOPLIN FAMILY/RICHARD HUNDGEN]

Janis had the first electric larynx. Her cry of love was in her voice, just as Jimi's was in his "ax." It was filled with all the cackling, shrieking, fuzzing, whining feedback of the electric guitar. Unconsciously Janis imitated the guitar as totally as jazz singers of an earlier age had imitated through their scatting the reedy sounds of trumpets, saxes, and trombones. Maybe that's why she was always so restless, all that static energy building up in her every day, like a 50-amp fuse about to blow.

"oh, lawdy, those dogs of mine— they sure do worry me all the time"

We become what we wish for, consummations draw us out. To fulfill them completely is often fatal. Janis perhaps listened too closely to inner voices pulling her down, beckoning her to withdraw from her family and friends into the goblin market.

"I'm a victim of my own insides," Janis said. "There was a time when I wanted to know everything. I read a lot. I guess you'd say I was pretty intellectual. It's odd, I can't remember when it changed. It used to make me very unhappy, all that feeling. I just didn't know what to do with it. But now I've learned how to make feeling work *for* me. I'm full of emotion and I want a release, and if you're on stage and if it's really working and you've got the audience with you, it's a *oneness* you feel. I'm into me, plus they're into me, and everything comes together. You're full of it. I don't know, I just want to feel as much as I can, it's what 'soul' is all about.

"I was in Port Arthur, and we used to listen to a lot of jazz and one day I was in a record store and I found a record by Odetta, and I bought it, and I really dug it, and I played it at a bunch of parties, and everyone liked it. This friend of mine told me about somebody he heard of called Leadbelly. He bought Leadbelly records, which were far-out country blues. Odetta was singing oxdriver songs.

"Anyway, we used to go to parties and play records and talk about poetry, and one day we were out at this lifeguard tower, we used to go to all the beaches and stay for the night, just sit on the beach and talk and drink beer, and we'd go to this old coast guard shack—a tiny little building. It was a room with four walls, all glass, you'd go all the way to the top and you'd look out on all this water and marsh, and we used to sit up there with a candle, a bottle of Jim Beam, a couple of Cokes, and sit around and talk. We were up there one day and someone said, 'I wish we had a record player,' and I said, 'I can sing.'

"'Come on, Janis, cut it out.'

"I said, 'I can too, man.' They said, 'Come on.' So I started singing a real Odetta . . . [*sings really loud*] Ya-la-la. . . I came out with this huge voice.

"They said, 'Far out, Janis, you're a *singer*!'

"I said, 'No, I'm not, man. Fuck off, man.'

"They told me I had a good voice, and I thought, 'Wow, that's far out.' And when I played records, I'd sing them to myself.

"When I'm there, I'm not here," Janis said later. " I can't talk about my singing; I'm inside it. How can you describe something you're inside of?"

Folk Madonna circa 1960 [COURTESY JOPLIN FAMILY/RICHARD HUNDGEN]

THE CATERPILLAR ON THE LEAF

"The only true wisdom," the caribou wizard Igjugarjuk told the explorer Rasmussen, *"lives far from mankind, out in the great loneliness, and it can be reached only through suffering. Privation and suffering alone can open the mind of man to all that is hidden to others."*

H. Osterman, *Report of the Fifth Thule Expedition, 1921-24*

the martyred slaves to time

n a drizzling late afternoon we land in New York. Outside the terminal we are balancing moments, waiting for the limos to arrive, as the afternoon stares back at us under an impacted dark gray cumulus. The atmosphere has the metallic odor of a motel room recently vacated, and the air is disturbed and buzzing with the thick hum of the city in the distance, the relentless murmuring of things turned on.

Underneath the huge cement arches of the arrivals building a girl with crinkly yellow hair is waiting for something. "Hey, man," Janis says in a disappointed voice, "aren't any of those guys going to pick up on her? That's *me*, man, sittin' right there, ten years ago when I was bummin' around, hitchhikin' here and there, hoping some cat would come along and take me off . . . or someone would at least feel sorry for me, let me fall out on their floor. She'll probably have to go through the same shit I went through before she gets herself together. Hey, man, *I'd* pick up on her . . . "

The temptation to tamper with time is almost irresistible for Janis as she watches the shy, defiant movements of the girl with crinkly yellow hair reading some heavy paperback, *searching*, longing and afraid.

You can almost see the thoughts running back and forth in Janis's head, seeking her former self through all the empty rooms and street corners of her past, as if she could just reach back and help herself around some bad miscalculations.

Finally John Fisher (of Love Limos) arrives. Janis is always glad to see him—he's someone she is always at ease with. Dressed in black, he moves about the car with demonic agility.

After checking into the hotel, we go out to look for somewhere to talk. There's a restaurant in the hotel. It is one of those incredibly romantic fabrications that are sanctuaries for "women of a certain age," intended to give the perpetual illusion of an untroubled afternoon late in the summer of 1926. Within, the ladies are tucked uniformly into little wrought iron tables. Janis clanks into this Ballet Russe rococo like Ghenghis Khan at the Court of Vienna.

The entire room turns towards us with a haunted gaze. Janis, out of perversity, wants to stay. This is going to be a *performance*, and the audience is far from appreciative. Mercifully, it suddenly reminds Janis of—perish the thought!— the Port Arthur ladies' bridge society. We decide to split.

There is a bar called Nobody's that is Janis's favorite nest, and that is her next suggestion. Myra Friedman, Janis's publicist rejects the place as too distracting. "Whaddya mean *distracting*? What you *mean* is there's too damn much *talent* there!"

We decide on the Cedar Tavern as neutral ground. It once had been a hangout of the abstract expressionists. Willem de Kooning is supposed to have knocked someone's tooth out there, or something like that. Anyway, in those days it was just a seedy bar, now it's just ye olde avant garde on University Place. This particular afternoon there's a sprinkling of demure hippies, but most of the men look like they had been to school with Holden Caulfield.

"This place looks square as hell," Janis declares, "but after a few drinks I guess it won't make much difference where you are. Am I right?"

There are some for whom the night holds no terrors. Among all these figures—criminals, insomniacs, whores, alcoholics, the inconsolable, the dreamers and lovers—Janis was the queen. At home in bars as anywhere, she always looked better as the evening progressed. The light of the day scanned her too cruelly, as if peevishly resenting her preference for the night. And she *dressed* for night in the outrageous costumes of circus performers, belly dancers, and opera singers—like some black Southern girls *who paint themselves bright as savages to stand out against the tropical summer.* It was only in *daylight* that she looked absurd. "With all those bells and junk tied around her," commented someone one who had seen Janis banging on the door of a bar in the early afternoon, "I thought at first that she was some college girl pledging a sorority." But on her endless night journeys, those phosphorescent costumes became her robes of office as she brazenly sunned herself in artificial light. A true child of the moon, she was its incandescent offspring.

is this person that's talking me?

I think it's time to order a few drinks at a time . . . [*Janis says*]. I feel better now. I was feeling really bogged down on the plane. I was talking with this doctor last week and he told me there is a pharmacology to alcohol. There are certain chemical reactions in your body that create energy here, exhaustion there . . .

I heard it's related to morphine.

Oh, no! He didn't tell me that. What he told me was—I ordered an Irish coffee and he said, "That's a Dexamyl." He said that chemically and molecularly—in the enzyme reactions and the whole medical shot—that it was a kissing cousin to Dexedrine in the way it reacted on your whole body. It's the same drug, and alcohol was almost the same as Miltown.

Changing states.

Yeah, I get tired of being in the same place. I hate boredom. I hate boredom more than anything. I'd rather be a junkie than be bored, and being a junkie is just about the most boring place to be.

That was a strange town, Louisville.

Yeah, that was far out. I haven't had a confrontation like that in years, like on the street. Usually, when I walk down the street there's four or five of them looking at me. But there was a *crowd*—sixty or more kids—across the street coming up and talking, asking questions.

That was beautiful!

They always are, man. I mean, you can't put down somebody for loving you. I don't think there's any performer who is that much of an egomaniac that they don't need those people; no one is, baby, no one. [*"Down On Me" is playing on the jukebox.*] First song I ever learnt. I'm getting tired of singing it. They made me change the words when I went into the studio.

Why?

Because they were all about God and shit, so I had to talk about "believe in your brother, have faith in man." Same idea, but not so gospel. [*"Call On Me" is playing on the jukebox.*] This one Sam Andrew wrote. He wrote some great songs— "Bye Bye Baby"—great songs, but every time we played 'em we fucked 'em up. So we stopped playing them. We started playing the easy ones, the fast ones.

How did you get into singing blues?

When I first started singing I was copping Bessie Smith records. I used to sing exactly like Bessie Smith, and when I started singing with Big Brother that was the only thing I knew how to do, and I used to wonder—especially when people would clap and tell me I was good—I used to wonder, "Is that real, or is that something I've learned to do with my voice?" But I think after doing it for a few years I got to understand that it all ties in. I used to ask guys I was balling,

"Do I ball like I sing? Is it really me?" That's what I'm trying to say. Is it really me, or am I putting on a show . . . and that's what I wonder sometimes when I'm talking. Is this person that's talking me? Does what I am saying correlate with my music?

Oh, yeah. Of course, it does.

I think so too. I actually think it's all me.

Well, its like in Kansas City, the second show especially, what you are doing is taking people from one level and lifting them up . . .

And insisting on it!

What happens? I mean, do you know the point where it turns around?

Yeah, I know exactly what happens, man. I was on stage and I looked out, and I knew they weren't ready. We were doing "Piece of My Heart." You know you can do a lot of different things; you know sometimes they get up spontaneously. Out in the Midwest they don't. They aren't supposed to stand up and they know it. It's hard to get 'em up. But I remember I was singing "Piece of My Heart," you know that "Come on, well, *come* on" line—well, you know the guitar solo that leads into that part? I came in early, and I walked all the way to the front of the stage and shouted [*in a hoarse whisper*], "Come on, *come* on!" and just fucking stamping my foot, and saying, "I'm not going to sing anymore unless you do something," you know, and they're going, "Whoo-ooo-ooo, yes, ma'am! Yes ma'am, yes ma'am!" A riot. Groovy.

All they want is a little kick in the ass. You know, sometimes I jump off the stage and grab somebody and say, "Let's dance." When they reach a certain level, you know, they want to be lifted, but they're scared. Then all you gotta do is give the old kick in the ass, a big fucking kick in the ass, man. Then the promoters get goony, turn the lights on, pull the power, but by then it's all over [*cackles*]. I dig it! I dig it so much, man!

I figure it this way, man, those kids living in the Midwest, like I was raised in Texas, man, and I was an artist and I had all these ideas and feelings that I'd pick up in books, and my father would talk to me about it, and I'd make up poems and things. And, man, I was the only one I'd ever met. There weren't any others. There just wasn't *anybody*, man, in Port Arthur.

There were a couple of old ladies who used to do watercolors and paint still lifes, and that was it. And I'd look at these books of paintings and go, "Wow!" and I'd try and paint that free, to let it go. I mean, in other words, in the Midwest you got no one to learn from because there's not a reader down the street you can sneak off and talk to. There's nobody there. Nobody. I remember when I read that in *Time* magazine about Jack Kerouac, otherwise I'd've never known. I said "Wow!" and split.

Kids from the Midwest, their whole fucking thing is to sit in row Q47 and be still. "I'll give you until eleven o'clock, and that's it." They get, "Do this, do that!" It's never occurred to them that they could *not* go in the army. They were told to go in the army. You know, it's a thing I do—not in defiance, it's a side trip—you know, I figure if you can take an audience that have been told what to do all their lives and they're too young or too scared or whatever . . . . I wasn't scared, but, you know, most of the kids brought up in that scene are. You know, "Daddy wouldn't like it." Or the South, or hey, man, California, but it's worse there, because California or New York, there are freaks all over, and they know there are other ways of life. The point being that out there they do not know there is another way of life. They've never seen a freak, and if they have they probably just think they're dope addicts, fuck-ups and horrible degenerate uglies.

If you can get them once, man, get them standing up when they should be sitting down, sweaty when they should be decorous, smile when they should be applauding politely . . . and I think you sort of switch on their brain, man, so that makes them say: "Wait a minute, maybe I *can* do anything." Whoooooo! It's life. That's what rock 'n' roll is

162

Graduation photo [COURTESY OF JOPLIN FAMILY/RICHARD HUNDGEN]

for, turn that switch on, and man, it can all be. I hate to tell you that it can, but it could be, and you're a fool not to try. I mean you may not end up happy, but I'm fucked if I'm not going to try. That's like committing suicide the day you're born, if you don't try.

When you're on the road it must be hard to make it happen all the time. Do you rely on things to get you going?

You mean tricks, gimmicks? Sure, I got a thing. I can't talk about it, but you have all kinds of tricks that I put at the beginning of the first tune to turn me on.

Like what kind of things?

Movement things, like the way you move, a certain instrument you listen to. I watch my equipment men, they know me real good, and they love me. So like if I'm feeling scared . . . if you aren't always on, man, then you damn sure better get on. I don't care how fuckin' tired you are, so I suppose in one way it is somewhat insincere. Like Mike Bloomfield, he only plays when he feels like it, well, that's fine, man, he's a very lucky guy. I've walked on stage bored shitless, on a bummer and everything, and walked off goony, so I don't think you can wait till you feel like playing. Sometimes playing is the only way you got out . . . . Sure there is an element of acting. I've been talking to Michael Pollard about acting, and I don't know whether I can act or not, but I can act like *me*. I can act like me like a son of a bitch. The most important thing to my performance is to kick me off. The more I find, the more I use.

That's the amazing thing about a great performance, that it can be very real and very structured at the same time.

Sure it's structured. Cause I remember when I was playing with Big Brother, sometimes I'd get so excited I'd stop singing and start jumping up and down. I don't do that any more because I know when it reaches a certain point, it's got to go here, and you gotta do it. Playing music isn't just letting it all hang out. That's like shitting . . . that's letting it all hang out, too! Playing is taking a feeling and turning it into a finished, tight thing that is readable and understandable to the people who are looking at it. It's not just for you, you can't just sing how *you* feel, you've got to take how you feel, sift it through whatever vocal chords you have, whatever instrumentation you have, whatever arrangements you have, and try and create a swelling feeling in an audience.

morning and evening of the first day

I had seen Janis perform in Panhandle Park and I had seen her at Monterey, but I remember her most vividly at the Summer Solstice in San Francisco in 1967. She was standing in front of this elongated forties airport car, smoking a cigar and drinking out of a bottle. Among all the fantastic images that arise from that day—sorcerers juggling red faces, gypsies, yage giants and self-anointed princes, clowns and Harlequins from the mime troupe pirouetting on the lawn, monks, and hordes of smoldering Angels, children naked as Adam on the first day of Creation, clutching balloons on the edge of a rain forest, Indians, wagonmasters, and all the flyers, walkers and divers that could be assembled in one place at one time—Janis seemed both the *most* fantastic and the most real. Perhaps it was just that among all the impersonations in the park that afternoon her emanation seemed the most plausible. It became her and she became it.

In the midst of all this insanity, a motorcycle cop, his boot on the running board, is writing out a ticket in all seriousness for "an illegally parked vehicle in a public place." As Janis catches sight of him, she taps her cigar and gingerly moves around the curves of the old limousine with the deliberate trajectory of a planet, swaying in that articulated gait that always made W. C. Fields look like he was trying to stand upright in a small rowboat.

I ask her if I can take a photograph of her with Big Brother.

Monterey Pop Festival, June 1967 [DAVID DALTON]

"To tell ya the truth, honey, I don't know where the boys went to," she says in her croaky little-girl voice, her face as serious as an old plate. I am amazed, but I notice uneasily that the fantasy is a reassurance. The image recedes rapidly, telescoping to a small round disk of light, as if it had been sucked back into the vacuum of time, leaving only Janis's ear-to-ear grin floating across the zero blue sky of the afternoon like the smoky trace of a Cheshire Cat.

The day had begun with little altars of twigs and grass at dawn on Mount Tamalpais, offerings to the local deities. The goddess of this solistice is a queen bee, and recollections of this day seem to hover around Janis, just as bees still hum over invisible tables where they once sipped honey. Janis did then, most of all, embody the spirit of midsummer. Sensual, ripe, fiery, dancing barefoot like a gypsy delirious with pleasure, she moves rhythmically to the accompaniment of her own daydreams, scarcely less amazing than the image of the Triple Goddess herself that Jonathan Swift collected at Lough Crew: " . . . an ancient, ageless childlike giantess, her car drawn by sparks of light who hunts the white mountain deer with seventy hounds that have the names of birds."

Everywhere bubbling powers of unknown valence are breaking into play. Hendrix clambering up onto the back of Big Brother's sound truck to shoot pictures with an Instamatic camera he has wired for double exposures. An agile, numinous figure mischievously alighting on the earth: "I long to be a shimmering silver light on the screen."

Teams of shouting, screaming, dancing children are swimming in the wake of the sound trucks. Janis, on the truckbed, is ladling out her raunchy blues like nursery rhymes. Little groups of awestruck kids stare vacantly at this mirage from the dusty area in front of the truck. A figure leans over the edge of the truck, grinning like a hookah. His features are distorted by the astigmatic focus of memory so that the tip of his nose is all that remains of reality. He is passing out

167

handfuls of joints that someone says were rolled from grass they planted on that spot earlier in the year. As the image of Janis and Big Brother begins to oscillate and decompose, I hurriedly attempt to fix its photomorphic details in my mind with R. Crumb's bold pneumatic outlines.

Despite the personal demons who later snatched Janis up and dragged her, like Persephone, down into the underworld, that morning and afternoon will always seem magically suspended, as if somehow removed from the onward rush of things and events, and at the center of this warp of time is Janis, radiant, earthy, and vulnerable as the moments that went to make it up.

As the revelers, wearied from wonders, like interplanetary visitors exhausted from their first day of exploring the earthly paradise, stumble, dance (the bands still playing) and blow themselves into the sea at the edge of Golden Gate Park, and as the great sun wobbling on the edge of extinction showers everything with flakes of rusty light, it seems for an instant that the original state of mankind must have resembled this day in its infinite possibilities, and that Janis, naive, filled with wonder and surprise, may have been its first beautiful child.

with "is she gonna make it?" in their eyes

One of the first times I saw you was at the Summer Solstice. All those groups on the backs of trucks . . .

Yeah, we walked over to Haight Street and bought some wine, me and Sunshine and our dog, George. We walked, sauntered, *sashayed* to Haight Street and bought some more wine, that's all I remember. I think I met Freewheelin' Frank that day, too.

With Freewheelin' Frank Reynolds, 1967 [JIM MARSHALL]

His book really blew my mind.

Well, some of them are real good friends of mine—Sweet William, Crazy Pete. Freewheelin' I met a long time ago. Moose is a good friend. I don't really know too many others, as evidenced by the fact that I got punched out by a bunch of them at a dance I played for them.

The trouble with the Angels for me is that . . . see, as friends, they are just people . . . but the club itself I think is inconsiderate. What I mean to say is, like, after I got slugged the guy came up and said, "Ya shoulda tole me who ya wuz." Well, you should be consistent! Be shitty all the time! Then you can be a genuine outlaw and be proud of yourself. My quarrel with the Angels is just that my chemistry works at a different rate.

When did you first come to San Francisco?

I first came in '62. I used to hang out in North Beach. I used to sing at the Coffee Confusion, sang there a couple of times. Sang at the hootenannies for beer. After I sang I got one beer.

It was the tail end of the beatnik era. There were still tourists coming around; it was an excuse to hang out on the street for spare change and some wine. I got beat up a couple of times. See this scar? Big lump from getting beat up by four spades. I'll never take a good picture.

Then I came back and joined Big Brother. That was one beautiful time, man. They weren't professional musicians. They were all friends, just people. We used to walk down Haight Street drinking Ripple.

These days Haight Street is so weird. Remember that *Suddenly Last Summer* movie where that guy gets eaten by cannibals? Well, that almost happened to me the last time I was there. I got out of my car. "It's Janis Joplin, it's Janis Joplin. Hey, give me this, give me that . . ." Pushing, pulling on me, trying to aggravate me.

I used to hang out in the park and have a good time. I wish it were that way now, but you can't go home again! We played at the Avalon because we were Chet's group, but by the time

HERB GREENE [2]

Above: Dave Getz. Opposite: Jim Gurley. San Francisco, 1967

I first went to the Fillmore, we weren't with Chet anymore. He was running the Avalon, and we didn't feel he could handle us *and* do that at the same time.

Anyway, it was some kind of benefit on a Sunday night, and Bill Graham sees us coming up the stairs and he throws us out. I say, "Why are you doing that, man? We're not with Chet anymore." He says, "Because you aren't any damn good."

Oh, he likes us now. He's good to any group that's made it

Tell me about Big Brother. I mean the people in the group.

Well, let's see. Dave [Getz] I'd say is the solidest guy in that group. He was an art teacher before. You could always rely on him in a kind of karma way. Peter [Albin] is more crazy than he thinks he is. He thinks he is very middle class and he just went a little goony. But he is really goony, man, that's how goony he is.

He wrote. . . .

Yeah, "Caterpillar," for example. "I'm a pteradactyl for your love."

If that's not madness, what is?

And James [Gurley], a beautiful, strong man. He never had any of that Indian bullshit, but he *had* an ethereal quality . . . I loved him so. We had a little love affair, almost broke up our band.

And Sam [Andrew] is like, you know, a very intelligent cat. You wouldn't know it because he's so good looking . . . One day I was on a plane, walking down the aisle, and, you know, everybody's reading *Newsweek*, the *Kansas City Star* and stuff, and Sam's reading a book in Latin! But I think Sam is a little thwarted in his music. I don't know why, but I don't think he's found the right way for his music to come out of him yet.

We were very close in a communal type thing, me and Big Brother. It was great to be playing again with them at the Avalon. It was such a gas, because I'd been on the road with a second group, and it just got worse and worse. And we weren't getting along, and the music wasn't together and we had to finish the tour.

Sometimes music isn't quite a *joy*, and it wasn't with the last group. Like Blind Faith, those guys didn't dig playing together.

So, anyway, one day I had some little time off, and I heard Big Brother were playing at the Family Dog. And I went over, and they asked me to come up, and I was so jacked that they asked me. And we hugged and kissed, and then . . . they didn't remember any of our old songs, and we had to make up one. They didn't even remember "Piece of My Heart." I was really *crushed*.

So word got around and Bill Graham decided to capitalize on it. He needed a name, and Janis was the name. So he got

172

The many (mostly monstrous) moods of Peter Albin [HERB GREENE]

us together again for one night. It was really just like a family reunion, man.

It was so much fun, sittin' on the floor, drinkin' tequila, kissin' and talkin' about old times. I remember walking on stage and saying, "It's so nice to play with friends . . . my people, man."

But you can't go back, right? I have learned from experience. And my experience is in my music and in my personality, and they have changed. It's like ex-lovers who don't ball anymore—we'd drive each other crazy.

I know I can count on them. If I get busted, I know I can count on them to bail me out. I know when James got into trouble, I was there. It really was a horrible, traumatic thing for him.

I guess the most upset people ever got was when you split with Big Brother.

They sure laid a lot of shit on me.

The second group had a little bit of that Motown lineup, you know, with a lead singer and an anonymous backup group.

I didn't mean it to go that far, to that degree. I wanted them to be a group, but it never jelled. This group I have now already does. I can't work with a backup band either, I need the emotion from the band. But I don't think it's possible to be on a San Francisco free thing with me and the band *totally*, because I'm in front, I'm in the spotlight, and if something goes wrong I'm the one who has to carry it.

Why was Sam Andrew the only member of Big Brother that you took with you when you formed your second band?

Because Sam and I sang very well together. And I thought we would really do well together, but we didn't get it on.

Now, John [Till] is what I consider a great guitarist for me. Shit, baby, he's playing a lot of stuff back there, you don't even notice. Like tunes we have to do—like, "Maybe," for example, that's got a dominant horn line. When the organist is playing the line, the organ is such a muted instrument that it really isn't carrying it. John's playing the trumpet part plus

174

With Sam Andrew, New York, 1968 [ELLIOT LANDY]

the tchink-tchink guitar part plus the pows when I want 'em plus the fills, and the booms and the bangs, and the pings and the ting-ting players and the bong-bong players. I watch him during rehearsal and he has to play lead plus he has to play the pattern. I guess all guitar players have to do that. I guess I never noticed before because I had two guitar players.

"One Good Man," you wrote that, right?

Yeah, it's a blues. Blues are easy to write. Just a lonely woman's song. Lookin' for one good man. And I've been lookin'. It's an eternal blues. About me trying to act tough, and nobody noticed I wasn't. It's like "Turtle Blues."

Who wrote "Light Is Faster Than Sound"?

Peter, Peter Albin. I wrote the "whooo, whooo, whooo" part though. See, with Big Brother it was usually a collective effort, except for Sam's songs like, "Call On Me," "Combination of the Two," for example. They really sounded like that when he came in with them.

But with Peter's songs, we would start with an idea, and

play it until it took form. Like "Ball and Chain." When it started it didn't have that much silence and drama. It's just that we played it so many times and knew it so well we learned to capitalize on it. One beat rather than four medium beats. It was, dare I say it? an *organic* product.

It's a lot easier to get your shit together, you know, at the Matrix or at the Avalon. You can fuck off there. You can be good, bad, great there . . . in front of your friends, and it's all just fun.

After Monterey and after New York, I stopped feeling that way. It's important how I sound now, it's not just for fun, anymore. Although, I *do* do it for fun, but, now, it's also got to be *good*. It can't be half-assed. They're paying money, man, and all that that implies.

They come to see you and you can't have an off night, even in Kansas City, because you are bringing a lot of people down.

It's a lot easier to get a band together organically at the Matrix than it is at Madison Square Garden where they are watching every note, every movement, with "Is she gonna make it?" in their eyes.

With Bill Graham [JIM MARSHALL]

entropy's terrible whine

To Janis, the unedited life just wasn't worth living; the mere succession of events was something to be overcome. It was an affront to her that all things and places should be equal before the indiscriminate rush of time.

Like most of those whom she admired and emulated (Zelda, Mae West, Bessie Smith), Janis felt that style was everything. It was something she had refined through experience. The things she had grown to be, what she made of what she was. Random events were humiliating and intolerable; they presented a very real terror to Janis. She was afraid of losing control, of letting herself be overwhelmed by the absurdity.

Janis did not find mere moments in themselves illuminating.

Janis: I hope you're going to edit this stuff. I don't want to sound like a senile, self-pitying chick babbling on and on about her days of glory.

It doesn't sound like that at all.

Know what's wrong with most interviews? They're always too long. There's more stuff than you want to know.

People who dig you want to read every word.

I don't think so. It's like going to a movie. Like *Woodstock*, I thought, was a bad movie. It had a lot of good footage, but a movie is supposed to exercise taste and is supposed to be made by an artist. It has a flow, like the way you write a story. It has a little peak at the beginning, a lull to grab you and hold you, and then another big climax, an ending. *Woodstock* doesn't have that. It just steamrolls through; never goes up, never goes down, never knows when to stop.

And neither do *Rolling Stone* interviews. *Cinéma vérité*, boring as hell. If you want to go to one, I'll meet you at the corner bar after you're through. And I bet I'll be feeling better than you will! I know that things are shitty, too—but I'd rather laugh about it.

San Jose, 1968 [JIM MARSHALL]

the great saturday night swindle

You wrote the "Kozmic Blues," right?

Yeah, I did write that one. I can't write a song unless I'm really traumatic, emotional, and I've gone through a few changes, I'm very down. No one's ever gonna love you any better and no one's gonna love you right. Maybe. Put you down. I like the song and I still believe in it to a degree, but I am still working on it . . . . I just realized, the other night, were you there? It's the first time it ever happened to me. I transcended the thing; I went into another stage, man. You know how on "Ball and Chain" I do that free-form ending, "Love is such a pain, love is such a pain . . . ." That's what this new blues is about. "Move Over" is about this man that I was in love with. He wouldn't be my old man, but he wanted me to love him. Men do that. They love to play that game, you know, taunt you with it. Anyway, at the end of that song it reminds me of an analogy of driving mules with a big long stick with a thing hanging, with a carrot on it, you know, and they'd hold those things in front of the mule's nose, and those dumb mules keep going after it and never get it. That's what I say at the end of the song. I keep saying, "Like a carrot, baby, baby da-de-da-dum, like a carrot, baby."

No one ever gets my imagery, that's the only trouble. No one ever listens to the words anyway. Fuck it. But I gotta hear it, I gotta believe it or I can't sing it. Anyway, "Kozmic Blues" was about someone who loved me. As a matter of fact, all my songs are [*laughs*].

That's the blues, honey.

Waaall, man, when do I get the other side? People are always doing that to me, man. Oh, man, it drives me up the fucking wall. People always come up to me, man, and say. . . .

I think you ask for it, Janis.

I'm saying, "Ooooh man [*wailing*], I did everything I could for this cat, I really loved him . . . he was just like a one-day thing, a two-month thing," it was longer than that in actual fact . . . you know it's like any kind of relationship where something hasn't worked out, you're sitting around—of course, there's two sides to every issue—but you feel *hurt*, man [*starts wailing again*]. "Oh, man, why? Why'd he have to go and leave me like that, oh, I'm so lonely oh-oh-oooh," and some guy'll come along and say, "Well, it gives you more soul." Fuuuck you, man! [*shouts*] I don't want anymore! That's life.

"It's only a magazine."

[*Sings*] "How much does it cost? It only costs a quarter. I've only got a nickel." But is it inherent? Do you really think it's inherent? Because I *thiiink*, I'm not sure, but I *think*, unless I'm fooling myself on one more level, I think that I think, at the very bottom . . . it's all a big joke [*laughs*] . . . on us.

The Kozmic Blues.

Yeah, the Kozmic Blues . . . . First of all you've got to remember to spell it with a "K". It's too down and lonely a trip to be taken seriously; it has to be a Crumb cartoon, like "White Man." It's like a joke on itself, I mean, it'd have to be.

But Kozmic Blues just means that no matter what you do, man, you get shot down anyway. Oh, I wanted to tell you what my new idea was, because I came up with it the other night while I was singing . . . I was talking about how love hurt you this way, love hurt you that way, now I just suddenly flashed . . . and I was writing a song about it, too . . . maybe it didn't hurt you because it wasn't supposed to last 25 years. Maybe love can only be a day and still be love. Like right now there's somebody being in love, then you *are* in love, you didn't get let down by love, you just have to spend the next few days and go to the movies! I'm trying to write a song about . . . not get it while you can, it starts off that way. I mean, get it while you can, and while you have it, you *have* it. The Kozmic Blues doesn't exist, unless you have nothing.

I remember when I was a kid they always told me, "Oh, you're unhappy because you're going through adolescence.

181

As soon as you get to be a grownup everything's going to be cool." I really believed that, you know. Or, as soon as you grow up and meet the right man, or . . . if only I could get laid, if only I could get a little bread together—everything will be all right. And then, one day I finally realized it ain't all right and it ain't never gonna be all right, there's always something going wrong.

The world is really a sad place.

[*Angrily*] I know, but they never told me that when I was young! I always used the analogy of . . . . I don't know if this is grossly insensitive of me, and it well may be, but the black man's blues is based on the "have-not"—I got the blues because I don't have this, I got the blues because I don't have my baby, I got the blues because I don't have the quarter for a bottle of wine, I got the blues because they won't let me in that bar. Well, you know, I'm a middle-class white chick from a family that would love to send me to college and I didn't wanna. I had a job, I didn't dig it. I had a car, I didn't dig it. I had it real easy . . . and then one day I realized in a flash, sitting in a bar, that it wasn't an uphill incline, you know, that one day everything was going to be all right. It was your whole life. You'd never touch that fuckin' carrot, man, and that's what the Kozmic Blues are, cause you know you ain't never going to get it.

What keeps you going?

Work keeps you going. Being here is better than going to sleep, I guess.

Is it the thing that's missing that gives you the blues, or is it the nothing?

It's not the nothing, it's the want of something that gives you the blues. I mean if you don't mind sitting around with no clothes on, why you could be happy as a loon. It's if you want to get dressed up, look spiffy, you got the blues. If you don't mind sitting in an apartment watching TV every night, you don't ever feel lonely. But if you want to be with someone and touch them, and talk to someone and hold them and cook

With Country Joe McDonald, San Francisco, 1967 [JIM MARSHALL]

for them, then you are lonely. It's not what it isn't, it's what you wish *was* that makes unhappiness. The hole, the vacuum. I think I think too much. That's why I drink.

It's a Capricorn failing.

What is? Drinking?

Yeah, that and thinking.

Drinkin' and thinkin'. I don't think it's Capricorn, I think it's people, and most of them think too much and they're all different sizes and shapes and they all figured it out. It all harkens back to when I was twenty; I figured it out. Got to get outta Texas, got to get outta Texas, soon as I get outta Texas everything's gonna be okay. I ran away once, got fucked up, came back. Ran away again, made San Francisco, hung around bars. I couldn't get myself together. I didn't have many friends and I didn't like the ones I had. Drinkin', sleepin' in some little nickel-dime hotels in North Beach. I was sitting in the afternoon in a bar, I wasn't supposed to be there, I was twenty, I lied . . . I was sittin' in there thinkin' and suddenly it struck me like a fucking light bulb. That's all there was, man. I would probably be sitting in that bar when I was eighty, saying I *can* do. [*laughs*]

I can make it feel better, you know, whatever, so I wrote my father this big long letter because I am very close with my father—I'm not talking about now, because I haven't been home in a long time—a big long letter about how you guys always told me it was going to get better, and I always thought it was an incline up, that one day would level off. And you know, you motherfucker, it ain't leveling off. It's going to go straight up and when I'm eighty, I'm going to die saying, "I wonder if I did something wrong?" Or some equally insecure, unaware trip, you know. I wrote my father this big long letter.

There was only one other man in Port Arthur my father could talk to. My father was like a secret intellectual, a book reader, a talker, a thinker. He was very important to me, because he made me think. He's the reason I am like I am, I guess. He used to talk and talk to me and then he turned right around from that when I was fourteen—maybe he wanted a smart son or something like that—I can't figure that out. But he spent a long time talkin' to me.

The biggest thing in our house was when you learnt to write your name; you got to go and get a library card. He wouldn't get us a TV; he wouldn't allow a TV in the house. Anyway, I wrote him this big long letter. And a few months later I'd gone home, and he'd already showed this letter to the only other intellectual in town—who was his best friend and they got together desperately and they just dug the fact that each other existed. This guy also dug me a lot and thought a lot of me. And my father showed him my letter. And when I came home this guy walked in . . . . This was all new and confusing to me and startling. I felt God had played a joke on us and I was pissed off and everything.

And this guy walked in with a sly smile on his face and he

reached out his hand and said, "Well, Janis, I hear ya heard about the Great Saturday Night Swindle."

I went whoooooh! I mean it's really true, huh? Here was a 50-year-old man telling it like it is. I was proud of that. I talked about that all the time.

Out of the jumble of my life, it's one of the few things I can remember clearly. I was always so stoned and, after a number of years, everything seems to run together. Certainly things that matter you can remember. That's why I should stop drinking, because I think I'm missing a lot of good shows. But actually I want to be able to do it and not have drugs or booze or coke be the reason I'm acting like that. I'm acting like that because I know how, straight. I never thought it would come to this. Something happened last year, and I became a grownup. I always swore I would never become a grownup no matter how old I got, but I think it happened. No sense worrying about it. Just rock on through.

What happened that made you decide that?

Just personal heavy changes. You have to do what comes naturally or it don't come out right. But people put me down for what I do, too. That's my problem. I do that too much, just put it right out on the street. But you can't change because you've become successful. Maybe it isn't wise though. Eric Clapton don't talk about his old lady, man.

Nobody talks about their private pain. Nobody wants to know about it, man. I used to think, maybe they just had better press agents than me and kept it quiet. But then I realized that it's me. I talk too much. I haven't heard anyone else in the music business have their sheet . . . shit on the street. *Sheet* on the street! Whew, tequila time! [*laughs*]

Something my mother used to say, "Janis, think before you speak." And I used to say, "Why? Why, man, because if I'm going to speak, why should I hold back?" Well, maybe there's something to be said for restraint. Maybe not in terms of truth, but maybe in terms of common sense. See, maybe all those cats wouldn't be so scared of me if I'd shut up, stop

With George on Noe Street, California, 1967 [HERB GREENE]

telling all I know, what I'm feeling—like that.

Janis, I think you should just keep going straight on. After awhile you realize you can't do anything else.

I realized it a long time ago, years before they even paid me to do it. Hey, I've met chicks who are doing me who can't even get a job as a stagehand because they won't change their style, take off all that jewelry, cover up their tattoos with makeup. They say, "Fuck you, man!"

They ain't changing. I ain't changing. I was just lucky enough people wanted it. But who's to say what can always happen? But I don't care. I may not be drinking port, but as long as I can buy my own bottle of wine, ain't nobody goin' to tell me what to do, man. Right?

Right!

Boy! I never said that before, but it's true.

Sometimes, on the road, I watch you getting ready for a show.

Have you ever watched me hyping myself for a show?

Yeah, it's beautiful, like the deep knee bends.

I do more than that. I talk to myself. I loosen up my body. Rapping on and on to myself. "Come on, honey, ooh, baby, blah-blah-blahblah, *uhn!*"

It's the same reason I run on when they announce me instead of just walking out there casually. I go whoooosh, so that by the time I get to the microphone my blood's going bump-abump-abump-abump. What were you saying, honey?

I was just going to say like everyday seems to be waiting for something to happen, something to get together.

You talkin' about life or about music?

Both. It's like when you're on the road, everything becomes very immediate, condensed.

Right down to the truth. That's why I can't quit to become someone's old lady. Cause I've had it so big. Most women's lives are beautiful because they are dedicated to a man. I need him too; a lolling, loving, touching, beautiful man. But it can't touch, it can't even touch hitting the stage at full-tilt boogie. So I guess I'll stop at this. I'll take it. Can't do without it. Gimme *that!* [*slaps, laughs*].

What were you like before? I mean, before you discovered that?

Wide-eyed, bright-eyed, and bushy-tailed. Just a plain, overweight chick. I wanted something more than bowling alleys and drive-ins. I'd've fucked anything, taken anything. I did. I'd take it, suck it, lick it, smoke it, shoot it, drop it, fall in love with it. "Hey, man, what is it? I'll try it. How do you do it? Do you suck it? No? You swallow it? I'll swallow it." There's chicks like that right now, man.

That little girl at the airport this morning, standing there in the rain, man. She reminded me of me when I was that age. Seven or eight years of doing that shit, man. It's strange, you know that? What strange, weird events took me to this place. Chances, strokes of bad luck. Bad fortune a year later would turn into good fortune. Who would know what it was about? The musical climate, events, falling out in that way. Every fucking conceivable thing brought it all together to make this strange person, this chick who was good at this one thing, man, just this one fucking thing. I lost a lot along the way. I may never get it back. But I know I ain't quittin'. It's just strange to think the kind of person I ended up, you know?

Everybody looks back when they're a few years older and says, "God, how did this happen? How did I turn into this person, man?"

Like when you see an old photo of yourself?

Yeah, sometimes I look at my face and I think it looks pretty run down. But considering all I been through, I don't look bad at all.

I think you look great, Janis.

Really, man? You silver-tongued devil, you [*laughs*].

You look healthy.

When I was a junkie I didn't look too good. You remember what I looked like in England last year? I looked this young, but I looked gray. I looked defeated. I kept it together on stage. But it didn't come anywhere near being as good as the first shows in Kansas City this year, because that was real. It was a boogie and they knew it. That's why I've been looking so good lately.

I haven't felt so good since the time I made it with Big Brother. The last year, year and a half, I've been going through a lot of personal changes. I was a junkie for one thing, but that wasn't it. That wasn't the cause of it; that was the result. I was afraid I was fooling them, and they'd find out. I think I decided just recently with my music, "Don't play it, don't lie it, if you're going to do it, be it! Try it! You're not *dumb*. Try, Janis!"

blues is an aching old heart disease

"By thy long grey beard and glittering eye,
Now wherefore stopp'st thou me?"
Coleridge, *The Rime of The Ancient Mariner*

Bobby Neuwirth arrives and Janis begins gathering up her feathers to leave. Conversations drift aimlessly, swirling about themselves, each submerged in its own liquid zone. A bearded man in his late 30's approaches the table unsteadily, as if he had just drifted in from North Beach.

Janis's travels are full of such enigmatic characters, and I realize with some alarm that we are in that vague world of repetition common to most bars. Like the ferryman who populates the adventures of heroes of folk tales, these mercurial, tutelary figures would approach her with amulets and advice—familiars awakening to half-forgotten roles and attaching themselves to Janis with the fixity of childhood visions.

"North Beach" slumps down at the table, bringing his own conversation with him. The labored syllables and exploding consonants give North Beach's words the cadence of nursery rhymes.

North Beach: Ya *know*, I never *heard Billie* in person.

Janis: I never did either, man. Course I was just a girl.

North Beach: I had a chance to see her, she made several appearances where I was living. Then I heard she died and then I realized I blew it.

Janis: I can dig it.

North Beach: She's now part of my music. Of course, you're part of my music now, too.

Janis: Shucks.

North Beach: I didn't know such a young girl could do it! [*Laughs*] Little kid like you.

Janis: Young *upstart* like me.

190

North Beach: Young upstart like *you*.

Janis: [*Seriously bored*] Well, we do the best we can. If you think I'm good now, wait ten years, boy. I'll blow your fuckin' mind. Whoooo! [*Stamps her feet and shrieks.*] If I ain't ten years better than this ten years from now, you know, I'm gonna start selling dope again, turning a few tricks on the side to keep my shit together.

North Beach: You took a coupla litta tips from *B*essie and *B*illie.

Janis: Musically?

North Beach: Besizes musically . . . you already have the tips from them.

Janis: What d'ya mean?

North Beach: *Don't fall too hard.*

Janis: I-don't-think-I-got-that-one.

North Beach: *Don't*-kill-yourself.

Janis: Maybe that's why you like them so much. I don't think that's why you like them so much, but I think it may contribute to the romantic mystique. It's intriguing.

North Beach: Are you as good as they are?

Janis: I know one thing . . . .

North Beach: I liked Billie long before she died. Bessie died about the year I was born, so I couldn't say whether I liked her or not before she died.

Janis: I can tell you one thing I know just from getting interviewed so many times, man. [*To me*] This has nothing to do with you, honey. People, whether they know it or not, like their blues singers miserable.

North Beach: They like their blues singers miserable and drunk.

Janis: They like their blues singers to die afterwards.

North Beach: Dying and dead.

Janis: Man, I've had interviewers come up to me . . . .

North Beach: There's no reason for it. There's no reason for it.

Janis: Well, I ain't doin' nothin'. I ain't doin' shit for them, man. I've had interviewers come up with a microphone to me and say, "Tell me, Janis, do you think you'll die a young and unhappy death?" [*Cackles*] Well, I say, "I hope not, man!"

North Beach: You know, you should be on WBAI—have a round-table kind of thing where nobody is out to ask you are you thinking of dying young or why do you drink so much.

Janis: Sure, havin' a good time, man.

North Beach: You sure do *drink* a helluva lot, don't you?

Janis: *What?*

North Beach: You do drink a lot.

Janis: I do. I do the best I can.

North Beach: You ought to watch it in the next couple years.

Janis: Oh, *man!*

North Beach: The pace. Slow down. You finally realize you're doing yourself in.

Janis: I figured that out a long time ago. I also figured this: I gotta go on doin' it the way I see it. Hey, man, I ain't got no choice but to take it like I see it. I'm a fucking human being, man, can you understand that? I'm here to have a party, man, as best as I can while I'm on this earth. I think it's your duty to. When I'm ready to retire I'll tell you about it. If I start worrying about everything I'm doing, you know— like this'll give you cholesterol or cirrhosis or some other dumb, unaware trip—I'd just as soon quit now. If that's what I gotta do to stick around another forty years, you can have it. Hey, listen, man. I plan on being around a long time, but that's the only fuckin' thing I'm planning on. Let it happen, man! I'm gettin it now, today. I don't even know where I'm gonna keep on rockin', cause if I start saving up bits and pieces of me like that, man, there ain't gonna be nothing left for Janis.

THE MILLION DOLLAR BASH

Let the reader consider what he would give . . . to stay the cloud in its fading, the leaf in its trembling, and the shadows in their changing; to bid the fitful foam be fixed upon the river, and the ripples be everlasting upon the lake; and then to bear away with him no darkness or feeble sun-stain, but a counterfeit which should seem no counterfeit—the true and perfect image of life indeed. Or rather, let him consider that it would be in effect nothing less than the capacity of transporting himself at any moment into any scene—a gift as great as can be possessed by a disembodied spirit; and suppose, also, this necromancy embracing not only the present but the past, and enabling us seemingly to enter into the bodily presence of men long since gathered to the dust; to behold them in act as they lived . . . to see them in the gesture and expression of an instant, and stayed on the eve of some great deed, in the immortality of burning purpose.

John Ruskin, *Frondes Agrestes*

is it rolling, bob?

"s this the bar car?" Janis asks, entering the room like an explosion, and everyone momentarily catches themself in an automatic reflex to the rolling rhythm of an imaginary train.

In the "Rally Room" of the York Hotel in Calgary, Alberta, a hundred musicians and friends are trying to dream back a recent five-day journey between Toronto and Calgary. From June 29th to July 3rd, 1970, to locate it precisely in time. Method of conveyance: train. Cast of characters: Full Tilt Boogie, the Grateful Dead, Delaney & Bonnie & Friends, Buddy Guy and his band, Ian and Sylvia and the Great Speckled Bird, Eric Andersen, Tom Rush, James and the Good Brothers, the New Riders of the Purple Sage, Robert Charlebois and Rick Danko. Everyone is wandering aimlessly about as they try to recreate the train's spacy timelessness in this institutional, square-shaped ballroom, like the anniversary party in a Czech film. The illusion comes and goes as groups of people stand around tables piled with sandwiches.

"We're only a handful of miles from Calgary now," says Sam Cutler as he slides aboard this imaginary locomotive. "It's all down to shortage of women, that's what it is," he adds, tapping into an unattached mood.

Janis is the presiding spirit of the journey, the Bacchanalian Little Red Riding Hood with her bag full of tequila and lemons, lurching from car to car like some tropical bird with streaming feathers, defying the sun to interrupt our revels with another day.

Janis's conversation is full of suggestion. She is familiar with time's sleight of hand, and ballsy enough to want to defy it. For her there is only one party, and wherever it occurs, that's the only thing that ever happened. The gears of time grind to a halt as Janis uncorks another bottle of tequila with its symbolic eagle ("He who understands has wings"). She knows that the greatest property of alcohol is its ability to abolish time, and with it its tattletale memory. Janis is the tutelary spirit of the evening as on the train, refusing to accept the conditions of adult life (that always involve some submission to the drab terrors of Time) by passing from childhood to childhood.

Janis's spell was always one of childhood, an ability to hoodwink the spirits of the moment and recover the lost Kingdom of Pleasure, not only for herself but for anyone who would set sail with her for an evening in her tippling glassy boat.

The feathers, the bells, the slingback shoes often looked suspiciously *mature* on Janis and like a child's put-on. Even the way she shuffled about in her pointy heels gave her whole outfit the effect of "dressing up." And so it was on this night that we all fell back for a few moments into the cradling rhythm of the train under the influence of spirits, songs, and Janis's great command of temporary disequilibrium.

The morning after the great *Million Dollar Bash* that took place on the last night on the train, Jerry Garcia stumbled out into a daylight as brilliantly blue as a constable's uniform, groaning in a parody of the amnesiac drunk, "I promise never to drink again, your Honor. How's my head? I need a lobotomy."

"I got the Dead drunk," remembers Janis. But even Janis cannot bring back the presence of the train completely, and the party drifts into dejected little groups. Rounds of songs start up again, and Janis, like a defiant helmsman, balances herself on a slope of the room as we guide ourselves through the treacherous crags and reefs of the present. On the choruses of songs, we pull against the gigantic tide with voices like overlapping oars, ghostly rowers gliding gently back in time.

Janis interrupts her juggling of moments. A sudden flush of apprehension takes hold of her. Someone is not helping to row this clunking memory ship through the heavy seas of the evening. "I want to see what these guys are talking about," she says, challenging Jonathan Cott and me across the crowded room. "Hey, man, what does *Rolling Stone* talk about to itself?" she asks, rolling us up into a collective proper noun. As it happens we've been talking about a Canadian candy bar by the name of Sweet Marie.

"Well, Janis, we were just thinking maybe Dylan wrote that song, you know, 'Where are you tonight, Sweet Marie?' Well, that maybe he wrote it about a candy bar," I say, holding the wrapper gingerly. "Is that what you guys talk about, really? Is that all, man? At least you could've been talking about *me*, you fuckers. . . . ' "

And, as if overcome by the hopelessness of *actually* reversing the order of things, Janis wails into Merle Haggard's mournful "The Bottle Let Me Down." In the corner, Rick Danko is singing some Miracles songs with Buddy Guy's bass player, and as the notes spill into the half-empty room lined with chairs, as at a high school dance, the participants in this extraordinary adventure take themselves off, aware that its suspended moments are gone forever.

> *Tonight the bottle let me down*
> *And let your memory come around*
> *The one true friend I thought I'd found*
> *Tonight the bottle let me down,*
> *Tonight the bottle let me down.*
>
> **Merle Haggard,**
> *"The Bottle Let Me Down"*

trains of thought

Time seems to reshape the things and events we have known into little clusters that move in constellated memories around a still center. Daydreams circle with lazy precision around certain memories that we locate in specific places only from convenience. At a great distance, like looking down an infinite thread of track, the spaces in which the original memories formed themselves begin to resemble one another, and must be recreated in a new daydream.

I can still see the train in its entire length with perfect clarity, as if it were an exact replica of itself. At any given moment, I can peer into windows that resemble the little glassine panes of clockwork trains, and examine its perfectly embalmed interiors—tiny lamps glued slightly askew on waxy tables with places permanently set with diminutive plates, cups and saucers, knives, forks and spoons.

Just now I'm looking through the window of the bar car. Janis and Rick Danko are listening to Eric Andersen, while on either side the plains of Saskatchewan spread out forever like a two-million-hole golf course.

Outside, the land is a platform of vegetable hallucinations. *Flatland* trees stunted by prevailing winds.

"That barn just yawned," someone says as we pass by a perfect red-and-white prairie farm. Its white loft window stares back at us in surprise like an illustration from a children's book. Or is it the drugs?

"You can get drunk just looking out the window," Eric says about the displaced sense of time and space that has infected everyone, like holidays, dreams, memories, utopias and songs.

toward the great divide

> The train trip wasn't a dream, it was a stone boss reality. I'm still on the train. I just turn on the switch, and the fan's on, and the train's still moving.
>
> Pigpen

The train is waiting for us at the Toronto marshaling yard, a slick modern diesel twelve coaches long with "Festival Express" painted in orange and black ten-foot letters on the baggage car.

While it is tempting to interrupt its progress (one irresistible moment—the mayor of Calgary, like the Pied Piper, announces to Festival promoter, Ken Walker, "Let the children of Calgary pass through the gates free!") there is a special pleasure in beginning at the beginning, letting the train puff laboriously out of the Toronto yard with its as yet unformulated contents of people and events.

"She's a born speedster, more like a bullet than a kettle," an old brakeman confides to us as we creep aboard as furtively as hoboes riding the freights.

Before setting off from the dimly lit station in the early hours of Monday morning, we are asked to sign a waiver which says in part that we will "keep the Festival Express from any harm or danger that may present itself," and for an instant we flash on ambushes by hostile bands of Sioux and Blackfeet or hordes of buffalo swarming across the tracks.

To look at the company of cowboys boarding the train it is possible to imagine that we're all setting off on some perilous journey toward the Great Divide: the Grateful Dead in their rodeo boots, embossed "Nudie" belts, sheath knives, and hoedown shirts from Miller's Western Store in Denver; James and the Good Brothers in Wrangler suits; the Riders of the Purple Sage decked out with the unmistakable ciphers of the genuine cowhand.

Once inside the sleeping cars given poetic names—Valparaiso, Beausejour, Etoile—the illusion of the Great Iron Horse pushing westward into unchartered land is destroyed by the stainless-steel-and-baked-enamel surfaces of the train's interior. Early arrivals are checking out the tiny sleeping compartments: "Man, I've been in jail cells larger than this," shouts a Marin County voice.

The little boxlike rooms with neat blue curtains stretch down the length of the sleeping cars like space-age opium dens. Each compartment is about 3′×6′ and a technological miracle. A galaxy of instruments and conveniences are insanely compressed into this tiny column of space: a large blue couch, a bed, a toilet, washbasin, jump seat, ice-water dispenser with paper cups, a drainless washbasin that uncannily folds away used water when closed, a clothes closet, an air conditioner, a fan, a cupboard and clusters of metallic outgrowths—ashtrays, hooks, handles, clips and catches.

All this compression is relieved by a giant window that spans the width of the compartment like an 8mm movie screen, registering the trees, lakes and rivers outside at 24 frames per second. In essence, the cubicles are both sleeping tubes and meditation chambers where the musicians spend quiet hours (between the orgies of music in the lounges) writing songs, practicing, rapping, getting stoned. The compact space encourages daydreaming, but its closeness forces you out into the lounges and bar cars to participate in what's going on in the world of the train.

The ingenuity of the room's design is also the source of endless Chaplinesque situations: bodies bobbing in and out of the compartments, bumping, tripping, spilling into the aisles in various states of mind and undress. Marx Brothers slapstick exits and entrances are reenacted in the early morning hours in comic desperation as stoned, drunk, wiped-out occupants attempt to deal with the sleep machine.

Getting into bed means stepping out into the corridor, because the bed, once pulled out, fills the entire room. But once in bed, using the washbasin or the john involves going out into the corridor again, closing the bed, using the basin and stepping out into the hall a second time to pull down the bed again. Given the stoned state of most of the passengers, any momentary forgetfulness about your goal could leave you hopelessly stranded in the corridor. As the Drunken Train lurches on, this mechanical ritual reaches new levels of high farce. Janis emerges early one afternoon about the third day out triumphantly announcing she's "discovered" the washbasin while looking for a place to hang her clothes.

On the first night aboard the passengers get to know each other in the dining car, where a buffet of triangular sandwiches has been laid out. The atmosphere is cautious, almost morosely quiet. Delaney and Bonnie play poker for octagonal Canadian nickels, and Steve Knight, Mountain's organist, bemoans the fact that he didn't bring his Monopoly set. "Thirty-six hours of this is really going to flip us out," someone says. The awkward encounters have the overtones of the first day of summer camp, where everyone hangs around waiting for something to happen. A subtle panic creeps up on everyone: five days stuck on a train with nowhere to go and nothing to do but look at 130 other freaks. Better to crash at any Holiday Inn.

A few people start to drift into the forward lounge. Leslie West and Felix Pappalardi pull out guitars. The mountainous West, toying with his tiny, ancient Les Paul Gibson as if it were a stalk of grass, lazily picks out a Delta bottleneck blues, and Mountain's drummer, Corky Laing, sings along: "Let it rain, let it pour, and let it rain some more. Got those deep river blues." Jerry Garcia, Delaney and his bass player, Kenny Gradney, join in. As the swarm of guitars picks up to a resonating hum, it becomes obvious what we will be doing for the next week.

From early Monday morning until we finally get off the train in Calgary five days later, the music stops only once— when everyone gets off at Winnipeg for the Festival. Buddy Guy's drummer, Roosevelt, immaculate in his flashy snakeskin suit, plays for two days straight, and it's a common thing to fall out, get up, have breakfast, and go back to the lounge to find the same "set" rocking on. The Festival Express is the reenactment of a piece of blues mythology, the box-car studio, where drifters like Bumble Bee Slim and Tampa Red, with harmonica and dobros, hopped the Illinois Central from New Orleans, or the M&O from Mobile, up to Memphis, St. Louis and Chicago. On trains with names like Panama Limited, Flying Crow, Midnight Special, Green Diamonds and Rock Island Line, the players incorporated the clicking steel rhythms of the train and the shrill "quills" of the fireman's whistle into lazy Delta harmonies:

Flying Crow leaves Port Arthur
Calls at Shreveport to change her crew
She will take water at Texarkana
Yes, boys, and keep on through.

That Flying Crow whistle sounds so lonesome and sad
Lord, it broke my heart, and took the last woman I had.

Washboard Sam, *"Flying Crow Blues"*

Seducer, Ark and mother (Mickey Mouse was born on a train), a verb in a world of towns, the train called others, too, just as it whistled Janis out of Texas. Bette Davis in *Beyond the Forest* heard its hooded voice beckoning. "Come, Rosa, come away, Rosa, before it's too late," the train seemed to say. "Chi-ca-go, Chi-ca-go."

"The train is like the guitar, man," says Willie Dixon. "You know, when you look down those tracks from the caboose? You see the ties closing up like the frets on the guitar. The further you get from the Delta, the higher up you're playing on the neck. In Chicago, baby, we're really wailing!"

As blue phosphorous lights settle on the marshaling yard, the Riders of the Purple Sage (Marmaduke, Dave Nelson and Dave Torbert, who form part of the Dead's 20-member family on the train) unpack their Gibsons, and blues gives way to country: Hank Williams, Merle Haggard, Kris Kristofferson.

Eventually people drift off and fall out. We wake up the next morning in the forests of northern Ontario: an infinity of lakes and rivers cut into a wilderness of birch trees. On both sides fields of daisies, trillium and buttercups curve up from the verge of the tracks. Giant copper-red boulders seem to squeeze the train as it passes through them. Sheets of rock, flat as mirrors, refract the harsh northern light that edges every stone and leaf and tree. Swirls and eddies of water wash around white tree trunks, half submerged, and islands that slope down to fine white gravel. There are so many lakes, it seems no one map could possibly contain them, and stands of birch and spruce so immense that images practically assault the eye.

In the lounge, a session composed of musicians who have been playing all night (Janis clutching her bottle like a baby), and others who have just woken up, is still in full swing. The images within and without multiply. Looking down the length of the car, the windows on both sides give the illusion of looking into a giant stereopticon that by some trick of light and space suspends the musicians midair in a landscape inhabited only by water, trees, animals and clouds.

the blushful hippocrene

Words, someone once said, are a halfway house to lost things, and in this daydream Jonathan conducts his interview with the train as it suns itself, like the articulated shell of some prehistoric animal found by the gloomy shores of a Canadian lake.

Cott: How are you enjoying this trip?

Train: Beautiful, man. The music inside me makes me feel really good. A strange feeling, though, you know, R&B in the intestines, country music in the chest. It keeps away that empty feeling I sometimes get on the regular trip.

Cott: Have you been keeping track of Janis? Pardon the pun.

Train: The Whale had Jonah and I've got Janis. A grand lady. As Eric Andersen said, "I'd give her my last sip." She knows how to survive. Gets up in the morning and gets moving. Like me. I can relate to that. My steam engine brothers didn't make it. But I just keep moving. Janis gets me feeling heady, like that old poem:

> O, for a beaker full of the warm South
> Full of the true, the blushful Hippocrene
> With beaded bubbles winking at the brim
> And purple-stained mouth
> That I might drink, and leave the world unseen
> And with thee fade away into the forest dim.

Sealed in that unstable zone of time where collapsed memories are stored, the moments flash past deliciously close, like the windows of an express speeding by at night. Each lighted window is the fraction of a sequence, automatically stored in the flush of a moment and waiting for us like a lucky hand of cards.

Yeh, that's Janis now, winking at the brim.

Cott: We'd like to find out about your origins, your influences.

Train: Well, it was all Asa Whitney's dream. I can't go back that far, like there's this haze and chimeras, something real ahead, and that was all Asa's dream. You know that it's just 101 years since that golden spike was driven into the rail at Promontory, Utah, where the Central and Union Pacific came together. But I always feel that moving through Canada now is what it must have been like going across the States then. Lots of people inside me today opened their windows, looked through me, and decided to move up here. Just look at the mauve and mother-of-pearl sunset up ahead. Just dreams to remember.

the angel's trumpet speaks and janis sleeps

The wheels of memory spin us back, and without hesitation the train obliges us by pulling on a pair of trousers made up especially for the afternoon as it strides jauntily off among a cloud of names. These little towns, some scarcely more than a huddle of shacks, that we pass through, evoke the mystery of unknowable places. The nostalgic transplants from the suburbs of London—Islington, Tottenham, Bayswater, Bethnal; the French trapper posts—Foleyet, Lainaune, Girouxville, La Broquerie; the Iroquois names—Kawa, Kowkash, Unaka, Minnipuka, Paqwa, Penequani; and the crazy wilderness names that trail into each other like a serial poem—Ophir, Snakesbreath, Decimal, Malachi, Forget.

Janis is in her compartment reading another chapter of her transmigrations. "Look homeward, angel," it whispers with the poisonous lips of the datura (Angel's Trumpet) that Zelda liked to paint in her madness, scorning the more obvious roses and violets in her Montgomery garden.

And there will be those who wonder, too, like the old woman on the portico in Alabama, "Where was she that she could not come back? Where did she go? Where?"

In another car a session shifts to an uptempo blues with Bonnie and Buddy Guy trading verses: "Knockin' on my door, don't want me around no more. . . . " "Forget it and let this trouble pass. . . . " Delaney's horns join in, and A. C. Reed

(Jimmy's brother) from Buddy's band pumps a fat Detroitish sound from his sax. The rhythm of the train is infectious, and by the time we chug into the late afternoon the sounds drift down to a slow boogie.

In Capreol a telephone-wire cat's cradle sleeps above the tracks, tract houses shingled in creosote imitation brick skulk around the station, and as we glide between the soot-black CNR oil tanks, the music grinds to the lugubrious shuffle of a New Orleans funeral band.

It is our first stop since leaving Toronto. Sam Cutler scrambles down the gravel bank to the dirt track that is the main road in Capreol. He comes across an ice cart being wheeled to the train, tests the ice, which is used for cooling the compartments, and heads for town.

Downtown Capreol is two open stores: a food store and the "Oriental Emporium Variety Shop," run by a Chinese family that sells Mountain Dew.

Sam happily goes off with an eight-dollar shimmering kimono of many colors and ten packages of Smarties candies. By the side of the train station and down a sand dune is a lake suited for beavers and black flies, intersected by a row of joining pieces of lumber. Bonnie and Delaney's sax and horn men play a lonesome Dixieland duet at the water's edge, while the rest of us skip stones. Six teen-age girls are standing by the train looking for Janis, who's asleep.

a kiss for the boys from manitoba

The farther west you travel in the prairies, the more squashed down and nubbed the trees seem in this unrelieved flatness, stunted by the prevailing winds. Grass grows up between the tracks.

Arbitrarily, we stop the train at Winnipeg, and, obedient to the willfulness of memory, the train exhales a cloud of steam and grinds to a halt.

Janis demonstrates Tequila etiquette. Calgary, Alberta, July 1970 [MURRAY SKUCE]

The Winnipeg Depot is a flat industrial area about four miles from the center of town. Brick and cement buildings—with facades of a displaced industrial revolution—stand in an open space overgrown with weeds; a monstrous 19th century pump behind a wall of green glass, a cement signal box, platforms and sheds. "Welcome to Omaha!" says Sam Cutler.

Jerry Garcia walks down the tracks singing a country blues. The film crew closes in, pleased to be shooting in daylight for a change, and captures a few solarized moments of the leader of the Dead.

"Believe it or not, I helped lay this section of track, hammered in these spikes right here," says Frank Duckworth, publicist for the Festival Express, making the anonymous stretch of track as vivid as a piece of the true cross. "People forget what goes into a track. They laid this section during the Depression, 75 cents a day for breaking your back in humid 95 degree weather."

Duckworth speaks almost laconically, like an urbane Bill Cody, but the words bring up a host of sweating images all reduced to this unassuming thread of metal that abstracts the 4,000 miles from Nova Scotia to the Pacific. He picks a squat green plant from behind the track. " Know what this is? Lambs quarters. You soon get to know your weeds when you're starving like we were back in the days of '29, '30. Makes a delicious salad and it grows just about anywhere. They used to feed us a staple diet of prunes. CNR strawberries, we used to call them."

The idea of the Festival Express, a train trip across Canada, is Duckworth's. He talks of the railroads with deep affection.

"Trains are almost all freight today, and it's a pity, because they were a very elegant, leisurely form of transportation. In a plane you have no sensation of travelling at all. It's like being pushed through a tube, a very sterile, inhuman experience. Imagine the opulence and tastefulness of travelling in those days. Did you ever see the carriage Queen Victoria travelled in when she made her state visit to Canada? Tassels

214

and velvet, padded and tufted like a case for the Czar's Easter eggs."

Janis steps down from the train, a blur of colors, as her red and blue bows gently brush aginst her face in the light wind. "Mornin', boys!" she says, crossing the tracks to the buses waiting to take us into town.

A local hippie warns us that the mood in Winnipeg isn't too friendly. "They're burying the chief of police today," he says. "Some guy shot him and two other fuzz while he was high on acid."

Janis, Marmaduke, and Eric Andersen set off for town and Tiny Tim's bar. Today is Canada's centenary, and Pierre Trudeau, the Prime Minister, is in Winnipeg to give a speech. Longhairs are shifting around the town square waiting for him to arrive, and Janis and Eric offer everyone a moment's unexpected entertainment by wading through the fountain.

The stadium where the Festival will take place is right next to a midway, where barkers entice the morbidly curious: "See the horror of the electric chair"; "the incredible half elephant, half pig"; "the body of a 2,000 year old man preserved in ice"; "vicious rats devouring a live python." Next to this exotic cosmos of freaks, a festival seems tame.

To add to the problems at Winnipeg a strong wind picks up during the afternoon, blowing spirals of dust into everyone's face. A sudden gust knocks the Good Brothers' drum kit right off the stage. It is like those sudden Midwestern dust storms blowing up into tornadoes. The concert ends with paper cups swirling off the ground in little pools of air. It seems that the currents may sweep us all away into another Oz.

Janis closes the show, and her set is remarkable under the circumstances. In the middle of "Maybe," a burly cowboy jumps onto the stage and asks for a "kiss for the boys from Manitoba," as in some scene from an old Dietrich movie. Janis obliges. As he's leaving the stage, this delirious embodiment of Manitoba thanks the stage hands for letting him through. "Why are you thanking them, honey?" Janis asks in her mock plaintive voice. "*They* didn't do nothing for you!"

every fool has his rainbow

Jostling down the corridors to the bar car or the lounge, as the train lazily noses its way through the pine barrens of Saskatchewan, sounds reach out to grab you from every compartment. Clark practicing drum riffs, horn players blowing the old familiar runs—Charlie Parker, Hendricks and Ross—Buddy Guy and a Cajun fiddler laughing and playing, the Good Brothers singing together in that old hillbilly way, Jerry Garcia and John Cooke (Janis's road manager and no mean country singer) harmonizing and exchanging songs. Janis, sipping gin, cackles away with some friends in her compartment, while in the next compartment, behind closed curtains, Flatt and Scruggs are playing on someone's cassette recorder, and everything is blending together, the tracks clicking underneath and almost above the music—and the train.

In the bar car, hardly as wide as most hallways, little groups of people swirl on egg-cup chairs, letting the evening drift over them. "Bring me another screwdriver, honey," Janis calls out, holding court, like Mother Goose, to a little gathering.

"I hope there aren't gonna be any operas on this train," says the bartender, looking up from his book, *The Rainbow Trail*. "The guy who was on from Toronto said there was a lot of noise."

"Nothing to worry about," Janis says. "The Who aren't on this trip." He doesn't understand, but Janis howls with a laugh as wide as Texas and he falls into it.

"Whoooh! There's so much *talent* on this train," Janis says, laughing at her own double meaning. "I *knew* it was going to be a party, man. I didn't take this gig for nothing else but that. I said, "It sounds like a party and I wanna be there. It's

Festival Express 1970
The Band Janis Joplin Delaney & Bonnie Buddy Guy Ian & Sylvia Eric Anderson Charlebones James Good Brothers Mountain° Grateful Dead° Tom Rush° Smith⁺ Sha Na Na⁺ Traffic⁴ Sea Train⁴ Ten Years After⁴ Cat⁴ Ginger Baker's Air Force⁼ **June 24, 27, 28, July 1, 4, 5.**

gonna be Rocking Pneumonia and Boogie Woogie Flu'. . . . Wow!"

"Holy cow, watcha doin' chile?
Holy smoke, it ain't no joke . . . ,"

Rick and Janis are wailing Lee Dorsey (Rick harmonizing with his favorite Dodge City whine). After a few more old favorites such as "I Kept the Wine and Threw Away the Rose," "Silver Threads and Golden Needles," and "Honeysuckle Rose," Eric does a song that Janis's voice understands intuitively: "Do you remember the night I cried for you, do you remember the night I cried for you. . . ."

"Are we in Calgary yet?" Janis asks as we hit the outskirts of Saskatoon.
"Whoopee," John Cooke yodels in his fine Western fettle,

217

"the next town we git to, we're going to divest it of its young womanhood!"

Everybody piles off the train and descends on the railroad souvenir shop, hungry for cultural trash: lurid magazines; sleazy paperbacks; candy-kitsch pastel emblems depicting beavers and grizzly bears painted on felt; postcards with Mounties, Indian chiefs and moose (legend on back reads: "Mounted, this fine head makes an excellent wall hanging for club, office, or recreation room.")

The owners can't believe their good fortune. A horde of freaks snatching up every piece of junk in the store! But to the denizens of L. A. and Marin County, Saskatoon is as exotic as Outer Mongolia.

Meanwhile, John Cooke and Festival Express coordinator Dave Williams make a run on the town liquor store. They slam down $400 on the counter. "Tell us when it's used up," they say, like a couple of prospectors come to drink up their claim.

The "claim" is hoisted on board, and the "People's Bar" set up. It now includes a giant totemic gallon-sized bottle of Canadian Club that seems like the symbol of All Drink and by the time the Million Dollar Bash is over will "prove the strongest man at last."

The party gradually drifts into the lounges. Janis spots a long-haired kid standing alone on the platform. "Get on, man," she shouts, miming through the window, but he just smiles and waves as the train pulls out of the station.

As we leave the town behind, the band picks up, rhythm gets a little faster. The wheels turn like a steel metronome, clicking off time as relentlessly as a Rhythm King—the meter of our thoughts, an invisible envelope of sound that infects everything.

The brushes lick the snare like a breathless hound dog as Jerry Garcia, Janis, Marmaduke and a choir of alcoholic harmonies wail into "I've Just Seen a Face," stretching out the country around us, pulling the words apart like rubber bands.

"I'm fah-ling, yes, I'm faaaah-lll-iing. . . . " When they get to the end they just start all over again.

"This is one of those endless songs," Bob Weir says. "If I could remember how it began, maybe we could find an ending, or we could just go on singing this all night."

Eventually the song dribbles off, and everybody starts singing John's melancholy imitation of Dylan, with heavy emphasis, which because of some internal structure of its own becomes the ultimate Beatles Beach Party song. While everybody else is nailing down the chorus ("*Heeey!* You've got to hide your lovaway . . . ") with alcoholic dexterity, Janis is moving about the lounge giving a soul lecture in a sort of counterpoint gospel: "Li-i-isten, honey, ya can't put your love out on the street, no, no, no, no, noooooh. You've got to put your love in a pot, honey, 'n' take it on home. . . . "

The effect of all this is beautiful and ecstatic despite the fact that the harmonies have by now collapsed completely, and the voices squeal and whine trying to reach the high notes.

The whole party looks and sounds like Merle Haggard live at Independence Hall on the 4th of July gone completely crazy: Clark Pierson wearing a Mickey Mouse T-shirt and calling out for a barmaid, Roosevelt wearing a beige-and-red striped jump suit styled after a pair of coveralls, Geri, a star of the Warhol movie, *Trash*, in a fringed green suede vest and nothing else, like an exploding green pepper. Charlebois's Cajun fiddler, Philipppe Gugnon, wearing his gray stovepipe hat. His long lean face makes him look like an Ozark Lincoln.

"Hey, is that my guitar, man?" Janis asks, sitting crosslegged on an amp in her thirties hot mama dress slit up to her thighs. Covered with beads, in her $4.95 hooker shoes, her cigarette holder, feathers, and the Stars and Stripes wrapped around her neck like a scarf, she looks like the personification of a national holiday being celebrated by a display of fireworks.

Someone hands Janis her Gibson Hummingbird. "I only know one song, honey, but I'm gonna sing it anyhow," she says, lurching into a "Bobby McGee" that no longer resembles Kristofferson's vaguely country folk song, now more like a gospel blues, while Jerry Garcia picks out sweet steel guitar licks that dance around Janis's raunchy voice. Everyone joins in on the chorus. "Bobby McGee" became the national anthem of the Festival Express and it must have been sung a hundred times on this trip, in bars, backstage, in compartments late at night, in hotel lobbies, and along the tracks. It seemed to sum up everything everybody went through on this journey:

> *Busted flat in Baton Rouge, waitin' for a train*
> *When I was feelin' near as faded as my jeans*
> *Bobby thumbed a diesel down just before it rained*
> *That rode us all the way into New Orleans.*
>
> *I pulled my harpoon out of my dirty red bandana*
> *I was playin' soft while Bobby sang the blues,*
> *Windshield wipers slappin' time,*
> *I was holdin' Bobby's hand in mine,*
> *We sang every song that driver knew.*
>
> *Freedom's just another word for nothin' left to lose*
> *Nothin' don't mean nothin', honey, if it ain't free*
> *An' feeling good was easy, Lord, when he sang the blues*
> *You know, feeling good was good enough for me*
> *Good enough for me and my Bobby McGee.*

Kris Kristofferson and Fred Foster,
"Bobby McGee", Combine Music Corp.

The Cajun fiddler with his chrome-plate violin is trying to play along, but he can't find the key. "Play the motherfucker. I'll back you," Jerry tells him, and he begins one of his backwoods reels, tapping out an incredible patter with his feet on an old suitcase to keep time. "Hey, this guy plays with his feet, *man*," Janis says.

"*Bon finis, bon finis!*" Janis applauds, as he finishes his tune. The fiddler beams. He asks her for a dance, and they twirl around for a couple of reels like two imaginary creatures from Edward Lear, dancing wildly by the light of the moon. Then in a sentimental moment he plays, "You Are My Sunshine," and his heart is in his bow.

Yodels and coyote calls ring around the lounge as he saws away like a fiddler at a barn dance. Sam Cutler charges through this impromptu hoedown with the totemic gallon-sized bottle of whiskey, like a screeching Redskin from Rimbaud's new-star-infused and milky sea poem, "The Drunken Train." He does a do-si-do around the floor and flies off into the inner reaches of the train.

John Barleycorn is king here. No one is immune from the deluge of spirits. The CNR cop is playing the tambourine, and at every lull in the music he shouts out a request for "Holly, Holy" by Neil Diamond. It falls on deaf ears. Someone offers him a joint. He walks over, looking like he might actually take a toke. "I just wanted to smell it," he says sheepishly.

It is the last night on the train and everybody is sadly aware of the fact. A number of wildly improbable alternatives are proposed, like diverting the train to San Francisco.

"We could have the whole goddam city turn out to meet us at Union Station," John Cooke says.

"Let's just refuse to leave!" Jerry Garcia suggests.

Talk of home, and everybody starts getting nostalgic. Free-wheelin' Frank and Janis's dog, George, Gypsy Boots candy bars, the ocean, movies on the late show, giant beds with silk sheets and all the minute familiars. Eric Andersen and Janis are singing a Hank Williams song softly over the hum, and its plaintive words drift in and out of the conversations like a sigh.

Hear the lonesome whippoorwill,
He sounds too blue to fly,
The midnight train is whining low,
I'm so lonesome I could cry.

Hank Williams,
"I'm So Lonsome, I Could Cry,"
Fred Rose Music

Things end on a comic note, however, with Rick Danko singing in his hokey country voice, as creaky as Chester in *Gunsmoke.*

"I've been in jail, and I got a sentence for 99 years."

"Oh, no, not 99 years to wear the ball and chain?" Janis asks incredulously.

"Yeah," says Rick, continuing the story. "So my old lady came to visit me, and she said, 'Son, but you don't have to think about this because, because it's the best of the tears.' And we all said, 'Ooh, ooh, ooh' and we all said, 'No more cane on the Brazos.' So I said, 'Captain, don't you do me like you done me. . . . ' "

The words become more surrealistic, stumbling over one another in their eagerness to finish the line. The evening comes to a close with "Amazing Grace" and a thundering version of "Goodnight, Irene" that is so loud it seems as if it will rock the train right off the tracks.

the soup and the clouds

Many musicians ended their day with breakfast and started again with late lunch or dinner, straggling into the dining car for the last call. It was one of the few occasions when sober, unstoned dialogues took place. The first meal of the day generally brought out the passengers' reveries.

Backstage, Winterland, 1968 [JIM MARSHALL]

"I could just lie in my bed for hours, watching the trees and rivers go by, letting collected memories drop on my head," says Eric Andersen. "It's only when you're drunk or happy that you have the courage to remember, and I just get delirious watching all this go by . . . silver, singing skies."

Tom Rush, in his snakeskin jacket, points out a lush green valley furling out of a lazy river on the right. Someone else sees a cloud in the shape of a giant's toe. Sam Cutler, like the jaded pirate he is, caustically denounces these romantic yearnings with a loud bellowing: "I've already gotten *over* the trees!"

For those who find it difficult to get themselves together after an all-night session, Janis always has some good advice. To a tomato-juice-drinking neighbor she suggests, screwdriver in hand, "When you're out of vodka, just go on and use some gin in the juice, honey. Really, it's the way to do it. Just don't smell the gin."

There is no caboose at the end of the train, but after a late lunch you can sit on the little platform at the end of the last car and watch the tracks trail off to the vanishing point. Although northern Ontario seems to be an uninhabited landscape, from this unobstructed viewpoint one can see elk, rabbits, moose, and the occasional human. Jerry Garcia reports seeing a large black bear scratching its back on a birch tree.

Duck hunters in an aluminum boat flash by on our right, a family on an outing in the middle of a field are frozen instamatically as the train rushes past. At night the wandering polestar, which is called the "Nail of the Sky" by Buriat Shamans, crawls across the universe like an incandescent bug.

It is at one of these late breakfasts, hung up between eating and seeing, that an unexpected friendship begins, a product of the train's cosmic calculus, and as fateful as any chance encounter on the Orient Express. And, after all, as Janis observed, "Chance is just the fool's name for fate."

As I walk into the dining car that afternoon, I see Janis and

Bonnie talking animatedly over a late breakfast. I think to myself, a little guiltily, that I would definitely like to overhear what is going down, but it's hard to find an adjoining seat in the crowded car. The only way I'm going to get to hear this conversation is to saunter over and pull up a chair—which is just what I don't do. To begin with, I am a little in awe of Bonnie's raunchy style, different from Janis's, but formidable, and I resign myself to never hearing this Epic Rap.

A minute later, I look up, my spoon in a lake, to see Janis standing across from me in the aisle with that familiar hand-on-hip stance and a predatory look in her eye.

"Hey, man, what kind of a fuckin' writer are you?" she asks in her amazing rusty voice. "Bonnie and I are having this incredible rap, and you're missing the whole damn thing, man."

"It's a private conversation, Janis. . . . "

"Don't give me any of that apologetic shit, man. Where's your tape recorder? You've gotta get this down, it's just gotta be one of the most far-out conversations that ever took place. This chick is really beautiful, man. She's as fuckin' macho as me. Can you believe that? Private, my ass, man. This is *your* gig, honey. You're meant to be *working*, getting your shit together, man. You're not on this train just to have a good time. I mean, this ain't *just* a fuckin' party, man, you know!"

Janis's attitudes about work and obligations struck me at first as weird and out of character, but it was a very real part of her personality, and after a while I began to relish the incongruity of her careening wild self, suddenly turning into this almost righteous Victorian matron denouncing sloth, carelessness, stupidity, and infirmity of purpose with evangelistic zeal. Everybody had their work cut out for them in this world, and, as indulgent as Janis was, she felt it was a blasphemy to cop out, fall down on a job, not get it together, or let something fall apart out of incompetence. It was almost as if all minute particulars of this inequity were crucial to the way things happened in the Kozmos. *Jesus Christ, we let the Garden*

*of Eden get away once already. We aren't going to let it happen
again, are we, boys?*

Although the source of much of this was obviously her
Republican upbringing and the absorption of her parents into
her system, in Janis these pieces had transformed themselves
to the level of myth. It was the sort of nostalgia for Paradise
vividly present in archaic peoples where all these lapses are
blurs of grace: slipping from a branch of the Kozmic Tree,
tripping at the foot of the ladder, falling asleep, losing one's
way. Original sin in endless repetition. "Hey, man, you don't ·
have to keep reminding me that we blew it!"

Janis was definitely an authority on this state of things,
otherwise known as the Kozmic Blues. All her bawdy accents,
liquid humor, and displays of courage could not shout it down.
In understanding that it is the sum of petty accidents that
have sewn us into our dilemma Janis guessed that *rightly to
be great is to find quarrel in a straw.*

symbolic wounds

Then he threw on the deck before
us whole handfulls of frozen words, which
looked like crystalized sweets of different colors. . . . We warmed them a little between our hands, they melted like
snow, and we actually heard them,
though we did not understand them, for
they were in a barbarous language. There
was one exception, however, a fairly big
one. This, when Friar John picked it
up, made a noise like a chestnut that
has been thrown on the embers without
being pricked. It was an explosion, and
made us all start with fear. "That," said
Friar John, "was a cannon shot in its
day."

Rabelais, *Gargantua and Pantagruel*

In the reflective present I return with the tape recorder. . . . All these moments about to be coded, set forever, the sentences preceding into the inevitable, like Pantagruel's sailing accidentally into a sea of frozen sounds.

We move from the dining room into the bar car. Janis floats through the passageways, as if a breath of wind had picked up somewhere between her wrist and her elbow. The flat honeycolored plains outside look apologetic by comparison. Nature at this latitude is little competition for Janis, whose landscapes are always more fluorescent than organic. Sultry Mother Earth, her eyes on stalks, peers at Janis through the window of the train, and then rushes off wildly to the right and left.

At the core of all this efflorescence is Janis herself, a four o'clock flower gradually unfolding as the afternoon revolves around her in the tiny bar car. Even the gaudy jewelry and hooker shoes cannot camouflage Janis's imperial dignity.

Bonnie slouches in her chair as casually as Huck on his raft. Pretty tomboy looks in Levi's and a peasant shirt, making wry faces at the past she serves up to herself almost accidentally. The sad times seem to fly after her and Janis in this half-submerged alcoholic state. But they extricate themselves swiftly in sudden torrents of laughter. Janis's unmetrical laugh seems to lead its own robust life deep within, arriving on the spur of the moment, a wild rampaging guffaw galloping to rescue an endangered flank.

No sooner have they risen above one sinking moment than they alight carelessly upon another, only to discover their resting place is infested with memories scarcely less treacherous. Two ballsy chicks railing against the unfairness of things, women is losers, ball and chain. But more than their brittle street rap what they have in common is the depth of their vulnerability barely masked by the cheap vinyl defenses they have wrapped around themselves. Tough, but melting easily, quizzical, petty, resentful of a host of wrongs and hurts both trivial and intimate, unexpectedly profound as well as ready to pawn off cliches on each other, slipping imperceptibly from state to state.

Bonnie whines and pleads with her own histories, extorting apologies from invisible defendants, and turns unexpectedly to tell a tale as poignant and innocent as Giulietta Massina in *La Strada*. As a little girl growing up in fifties Alabama, her mother took her to see this black gospel singer at a tiny local club. She was mesmerized, as unable to move as someone who has witnessed a vision. She asked her mother if she could go up to the man and touch him. As she put her little hand on his arm, he turned and looked at her. And from that day on she felt possessed.

Janis [*to waiter*]: Screwdriver.

Bonnie: Scotch and Coke.

Janis: I've got lots of tie-dyed velvet. . . . I had these tie-dyed satin sheets, the most beautiful fuckin' sheets in the world, and I started makin' it with this cowboy and he shredded them up with his cowboy boots [*laughs, ice tinkling*]. Three hundred dollar satin sheets shredded by cowboy boots. I loved every minute of it.

Bonnie: Is that true?

Janis: It is true, man, they're ruined.

Bonnie: Now, that dude can't've been that good.

Janis [*cracks up*]: Well, how do you see it so far, David?

David: It's a gas.

Janis: So do I. To tell you the truth, man, I've woken up a lot. . . . Listen, I didn't take this gig . . . the money ain't that great. I didn't take this gig for any reason other than this party, man. I said it sounds like a party, man, and I wanta be there. My band's picking us up in Winnipeg, and the Band is picking us up in Winnipeg. And I'm gonna pick one of them up in Winnipeg!

Bonnie: Hey, did you see our organ player? His name is Jim Gordon. And, Janis, I swear to God, Rick and Robbie were there. For ten years I worked with him. . . . [*catches a look on Janis's face*] Oh, yeah, you read that article, huh? [*Janis cackles.*] I knew you'd read it. I read it too . . . .

Janis: The chick's beautiful, man . . . How old are you? What sign are you?

Bonnie: I'm twenty-five.

Janis: Gosh, you're younger than me.

Bonnie: You're twenty-seven right?

Janis: You seem as old as me.

Bonnie: I am as old as you. I'm older than you.

Janis: I've been on the streets ten years.

Bonnie: *I've* been on the streets ten years—you ain't got that on me—I've been there, too.

Janis: I knew you looked good. You just fired your old band, didn't you?

Bonnie: No, our old band just quit. They wanted to pick with Joe Cocker.

Janis: All those eighty-five people? When I saw Joe Cocker at the Fillmore West and I read in *Rolling Stone* he had an eighty-five piece group. . .children, dogs, musicians, and he brings all life on stage. I went down to the Fillmore, and Bill Graham didn't let no one on stage but the musicians—he made all the chicks, all the babies, all the dogs, stand on the side. Because if he's singing and if he's playing music, he's playing music. He ain't talking about a life style, he ain't philosophizing. He's playing music. And he ought to get musicians up there and play the shit. If he wants groupies, he can get 'em after the show.

Bonnie: You can get them local, man. You don't have to bring them. My girlfriend told me that she got in a fight with her girlfriend because her girlfriend said that she read in *Rolling Stone* that someone was supposed to have seen me yelling to them, "You dirty motherfuckers! You stole my band," and all this shit. It made me really mad because I really love my musicians.

Janis: Did you lose that great organ player?

Bonnie: Bobby Whitlock. Man, he's in England with Eric. There's a million and one musicians in this world that's never even been heard of that can just kick ass.

Bonnie: Yeah, so as far as your musical ability, we can always find other musicians. But I love those guys and it really did crush me, but I was cool. And it hurt me and it killed me. But I was cool! And it's a lie that I said it. It may not be a lie what I thought. I was crushed. I can admit it now we have a new band. We're together. In the meantime, you know Bobby Keys, that great sax player. He had no gigs, man, because they let him down. Eric told him he could come over to England and make a lot of bread doing sessions. And he believed him. So now he says he can't pay for the plane. So, in the meantime, he's sitting home with no gigs. Because I'm not going to fire the new band.

Janis: I've worked with three bands, four including when I was a kid, but three pro bands. We got on stage and did it anyway under the lights, but those boys really help you. The singer is only as good as the band, and this is the first band that really helped me. I got a drummer, man, that drives me up the wall, I wanna tell you. I was doing this shit in a tune last week. You know how you have verse, bridge, verse, and then you have a vamp? The vamp is free, it's Janis. Janis gets to sing or talk or walk around the stage and act foxy, whatever she wants to do, right? It's free, and all the band is supposed to do is keep up the groove. So I was singing, "Well I told that man, I said baby, I said baby, I said baby. . . . " I went up in thirds. And when I hit that high "baby," I did a kick with my ass to the right, the drummer went bam! with a rim shot. And I turned around and said, "My God, where did you learn that part, man? I just made it up a minute ago."

I walked off stage and said, "Where did you learn to play behind singers like that?" And he said, "I used to back strippers." That's how you learn to play, man.

Bonnie: Watch that ass. When it's going to the right, you hit a rim shot. That's exactly what I tell my drummer.

David: Clark is a great drummer.

Janis: He's not subtle, but he's all right. Right on. I guess that's what I need. I ain't real subtle either, to tell the truth.

Bonnie: When you listen to your band, what do you listen to the most?

Janis: Drums and bass.

Bonnie: I know. Me too. Drums and bass. It's the bottom; it's the rhythm.

Janis: That's what kicks you.

Bonnie: Since you are a lead instrument yourself. Everyone wants to play their own ax, like the greatest guitar player. You listen immediately to the bottom. You're the lead instrument, so all you need is rhythm. You listen immediately to the bottom.

Janis: All you need is the bottom, the middle you just count on to fill in, but what you need is that kick in your ass, man.

Bonnie: Because you know you're gonna do your lead right as long as your bass and drummer are together.

Janis: If you get the kick in the ass. You hear it when they're great. But mostly I'm so involved with the song that I don't even hear the band, you know what I mean? All I hear is when they're wrong. When they're right, I just keep singing and talking my shit and telling my stories. But as soon as someone does something wrong, man, I get goony.

Bonnie: When you're rapping and all of a sudden they hit a hum, dum, dum, into another groove. And you ain't ready for it, you turn around and look at that drummer and bass player. Jim Keltner used to get so mad at me. He'd say, "Why do you turn around and give me dirty looks?" That's no dirty look, that's my face.

Janis: That's when you were in the wrong place when I was in the other place.

Bonnie: I was here and you were there. And you're not supposed to be nowhere that I ain't.

Janis: That's what I dig about the group I got now. I had groups that learned the tunes, learned the stops, learned whatever-the-fuck. This band, man, I could be in the middle of a verse and go on a different trip, and they can follow me.

They won't go with the arrangement. They go right with me, man. Like if I decide to extend the verse for 8 bars, 16 bars, whatever the bars are called? When I get through saying something, I ain't through so I keep talkin'. They don't quit. They know I'm not through, so they keep playing.

Bonnie: I used to do the exact same thing with Delaney. I'd never keep my eyes off him, because you never know what he's gonna do. He might want to tell his life story.

Janis: I do it all the time.

Bonnie: I do it too. I tell my life story every show I do.

Janis: Sometimes I wonder if they're worth it, man. If they're worth all that fuckin' grief that they drag out of you. But you can't think about it in those terms, right?

Bonnie: The only thing I wonder about is, not if they're worth it, but if they understand it. Because I hate to expose myself completely and have it go this far over their heads. Because that's what you're doing, you're taking off completely the whole plastic down from the front of you. You might as well just get nude, because you're completely exposing your inside feelings. It's reality, it's not a show when you really get into it as much as that. I really get uptight. Not at what they yell, it's just that they shouldn't yell anything at all. What I want to hear from that audience is understanding.

I don't want to hear someone yell, "Where's Clapton?" I'm standin' up there, I got three children and it's very hard for me to go off and leave them. That's part of me. And I'm not saying it! I'm giving up someone who really belongs to me, because this is something I have to do as a complete individual. But they are individuals, too, so I can't subject them to my life—it's their own choice. I don't get them high, I don't get high in front of them. I don't want to give them mescaline. That's their own choice.

I wish I could take that tape from Germany, because we never played so hot. And they were yelling, "boo, hiss." They yelled from the minute we hit that stage with Eric. Because they figured Eric was going to have his own shit. Eric Clapton

with Delaney and Bonnie and Friends. It looks like there's Eric Clapton's group, and then there's Delaney and Bonnie. They didn't think he was going to play with us. I have no pride. It hurt my feelings. I cried. And I couldn't do any more than four numbers. Because I'm not going to cram anything down anyone's throat who don't dig it. You're completely putting the whole plastic shield down and exposing your whole inner feelings to everyone. This is the only way I can get release from what I feel. You gotta talk. You gotta tell. And I have the God-given talent to be able to do that. I don't have to live in a plastic shell all my life. And I think it should be appreciated. And if you don't like it, I think you should get your money and split. And if people writing about it don't dig it, they have no business interviewing me. Let them interview someone they like, because if you don't have something nice to say, don't write about that person.

Janis: I had a couple of shows where I played the whole show really into it, completely giving all I had, man, and I was doing a free-form thing: talking, bringing it all out, letting it all go, man. Just talking about Janis and all the men that hurt her, and all the men that maybe she let down. And everything that you got to say, man, all of a sudden it starts coming out of your mouth, and you didn't even intend it to. And all of a sudden I heard them speak, I heard them talking in the middle of my fucking shit, man, and I stopped and I waited to see if they'd quit.

Bonnie: It's like a sledgehammer in your chest, man.

Janis: They didn't quit. And I grabbed the microphone and said, "I ain't cryin my ass for you, man." I put the microphone down and walked off the stage. I blew my contract and all that shit. But fuck that, man. I ain't gonna get out there and cry my soul out for people that are talking about: "How's your brother? Did you get laid on Thursday? That's a cute dress!" I'm up there talking about my pain. Fuck you, man.

Bonnie: Our pain is common. You know the feeling that a woman has—it's very hard for a man to get to a woman because they take it in different ways. It's like a woman can understand another woman. And everyone has been in love and been turned down. And everyone has had someone who really loved them that they just didn't love. And what are you going to do? You don't want to hurt him, but you just don't love him. And that's hurt and that's pain. So you're telling that to people, and there's a lot of people that can relate to that. In the meantime, Joe Shmoe is assin' off, and you're being very serious. And people say, "Delaney walked off stage! He thinks he's so hot!" He's exposing himself, and everyone's laughing. They're ignoring him, ignoring his whole soul. It's really ugly to do. Because everyone, in the meantime, is talking about understanding and loving one another and peace and let's talk about it, let's be truthful with each other. And here's someone on a platform in front of thousands of people. There's probably 45,000 that understand, that have been through that. And then there're the others that have maybe been through that, but don't even want to look at it. So they schmaltz it up for everyone else. And if it so happens that they're sitting in the front row, and you're trying to do something. . . . If you were Frank Sinatra you could look up to the left light or the right light, but I gotta look my people in the eye.

Bonnie: Why did they spend their money to come there?

Janis: It's the fifties against the sixties. In the fifties they used to sing songs because they had nice tunes and they had nice melodies. They didn't hear the words. They were nice to foxtrot to or something.

Right now it's different for a guitar player because he's playing D minor, F whatever-the-fuck, but I'm up there saying, "I feel, you know, I hurt, please help." I'm saying *words*, man, and if I look at an audience and they ain't understanding me, it's just like getting kicked in the teeth.

Bonnie: As much money as Las Vegas has, they ain't got enough for me. They gonna have to come up with a lot of bread.

Janis: I turned them down, too. Do you know what's very

strange, bizarre? Seven or eight years from now the people going to Las Vegas will be fans of ours—they're gonna have grown up and they're gonna be going to Las Vegas. In ten years, honey, it's gonna be our crowd, man. We can go back there and rock 'n' roll . The sixties are selling now in Las Vegas. Ten years from now the seventies are gonna be selling. And if the Jefferson Airplane still manage to keep their dregs together, they're gonna be playing there, too.

Bonnie: I certainly hope you're right, man, because I had a super bummer in Las Vegas.

Janis: I went there once. I checked into this motel and they gave me a coupon worth a dollar at the roulette table, a dollar in quarters at the slot machine and a coupon worth two drinks. I played a dollar's worth of roulette and I lost. I had two free drinks and said, "Fuck 'em." I came out of there stoned anyway. They asked me, "How did you learn to sing the blues like that? How did you learn to sing that heavy?" I didn't learn shit, man. I just opened my mouth and that's what I sounded like, man. You can't make up something that you don't feel. Bonnie, she's a bitchin' singer. You know she ain't making up nothing. That chick's a woman, man. I don't know what kind of dues she's paying, but she's paid them; she's still paying them. She's an honest-to-God real life woman, man, or she wouldn't be able to sound like that. I didn't make it up. I just opened my mouth and it existed.

Bonnie: You know that a lot of people say the trouble with women is they don't think about what they say before they say it.

Janis: That's the good thing about women, man. Because they sing their fuckin' insides, man. Women, to be in the music business, give up more than you'd ever know. She's got kids she gave up . . . . Any woman gives up home life, an old man probably. You give up a home and friends, children and friends. You give up an old man and friends, you give up every constant in the world except music. That's the only thing in the world you got, man. So for a woman to sing, she really needs to or wants to. A man can do it as a gig, because he knows he can get laid tonight.

Bonnie: A lot of musicians are married and worship the footsteps their wives walk in. But they go on the road and they ball, and they have a ball. But when they are home, no one is going to break their marriage up, there ain't nobody gonna hurt their children. But what man would have you and let you do what you must do?

Janis: That's the trouble! You either got to be as big a star as the chick or you got to be a flunky. And no woman, at least me, I don't want an ass-kisser. I want a cat that's bigger and stronger and ballsier than me. When I'm pulling my shit as a singer it's hard to find him, because the only cats that hang around dressing rooms are flunkies. They're all right for a night, but when you want to talk about a man, ain't no man in the world needs to hang around a dressing room. The men are out in some log cabin growing grass and chopping trees, and I never get to see them. But that gives you more soul, right?

Bonnie: When Delaney and I met, it was that fast. I married him seven days after I met him. I was never married before, I was twenty-three. He was never married and twenty-six and no one even thought about getting married. For ten years before I met Delaney, I lived in hell. I worked in strip joints and truck stops, and I went on between the second-best and the best stripper. You got to have a break so the star could come out. I'd be out there singing a song and they'd be yelling, "Take it off, baby!"

Janis: I wasn't even a chick singer until I became a chick singer. I was a dope dealer and a hang-out artist. And a chick on the street trying to find a place to sleep and a cat to lay. I didn't ever sing until they turned me into a rock 'n' roll singer. I sang for free beer once in a while, but I never even wanted to grow up to be a singer. It was a very bizarre experience.

Bonnie: It's really weird. I never wanted to be anything

240

else. That was my whole life.

Janis: All my life I just wanted to be a beatnik. Meet all the heavies, get stoned, get laid, have a good time. That's all I ever wanted. Except I knew I had a good voice and I could always get a couple of beers off of it. All of a sudden someone threw me in this rock 'n' roll band. They threw these musicians at me, man, and the sound was coming from behind. The bass was charging me. And I decided then and there that that was it. I never wanted to do anything else.

It was better than it had been with any man, you know. Maybe that's the trouble.

With George at Noe Street apartment. San Francisco, 1967 [JIM MARSHALL]

(Outrageously) at home. Larkspur, California, 1970 [AP/WIDE WORLD PHOTOS]

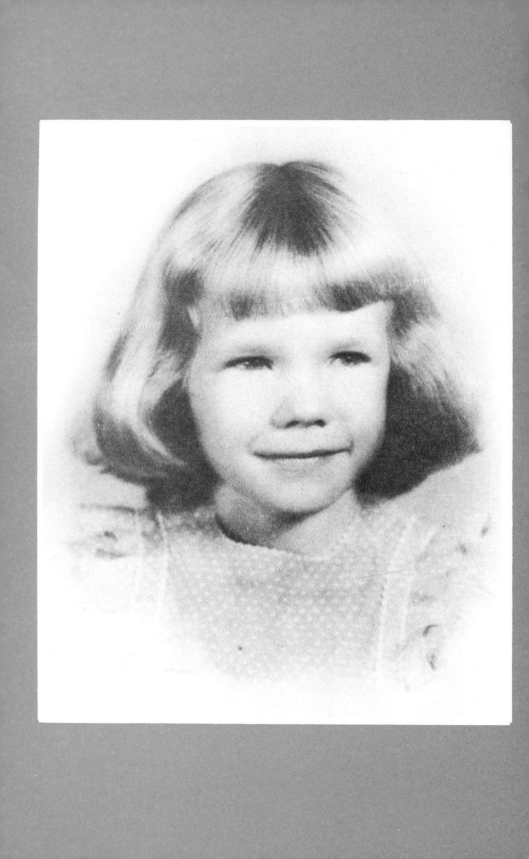

A
CHRONOLOGY

All those things—family, native land—are perhaps more attractive in the imaginations of such people as us, who pretty well do without native land or family either, than they are in reality. I always feel I am a traveller, going somewhere and to some distant destination.

If I tell myself that the somewhere and the destination do not exist, that seems to me very reasonable and likely enough.

Vincent Van Gogh, *August 1888, in a letter*

a chronology

1943   *JANUARY 19. 9:45 a.m. Janis Lyn Joplin born to Seth and Dorothy Joplin at St. Mary's Hospital, Port Arthur, Texas.*

1950   *Joins the Bluebirds.*

Begins to exhibit antisocial and rebellious behavior.

1958   *Reads about Kerouac and the Beats in* Time *magazine.*

1960   *JUNE. Graduates from Thomas Jefferson High. Enrolls at Lamar College in nearby Beaumont.*
SUMMER. Attends Lamar Tech College. Visits Houston, hangs around folk coffeehouses.
Goes to Los Angeles, works as a key punch operator and hangs out in Venice, California. Falls in with local beatnik scene. FALL. Returns to Port Arthur in sheepskin jacket to "spread the word."

1961   *NEW YEAR'S EVE. Has first public singing engagement at the Halfway House in Beaumont.*
1962   *JANUARY. Begins singing at the Purple Onion in Houston. Records a jingle, "This Bank Is Your Bank," for a bank in Nacogdoches. Classes at Lamar Tech.*
SUMMER. Waitress in a bowling alley. Hangs out at Louisiana bars across the river. Leaves with Jack Smith for Austin and moves into folk/beat apartment house known as the Ghetto. Enrolls in Fine Arts Program at the University of Texas in Austin. Sings, accompanying herself on autoharp, as part of

*local bluegrass band, the Waller Creek Boys
(Powell St. John on harmonica and Larry
Wiggins on bass) at the Union Building on
Sunday afternoons and at Threadgill's Bar
& Grill, a converted gas station, on
Wednesday evenings. Repertoire consists of
Leadbelly, Bessie Smith, Jean Ritchie, Rosie
Maddox and bluegrass.
FALL. Dealing grass on campus,
experimenting with peyote and taking massive
doses of seconal. Voted "Ugliest Man on
Campus." Chet Helms, an old Austin
acquaintance, returns from San Francisco
and tells her about the post-Beat scene.*

Kenneth Threadgill

1963   *JANUARY 23. Hitches to San Francisco with Chet. Two days later is singing in North Beach (San Francisco) coffeehouses, passing the hat for beers. Often sings a cappella at the Coffee Confusion and the Coffee Gallery, occasionally accompanied by Jorma Kaukonen (future guitarist with Jefferson Airplane). Sings Bessie Smith and Ma Rainey blues with folksingers Roger Perkins and Larry Hanks. Hangs out with David Crosby and Nick Gravenites. Lives off passing the hat, part-time jobs and unemployment. Begins drinking heavily, also taking speed. Meets Peter Albin, future bass player for Big Brother (played with J. P. Pickens in a "progressive" bluegrass band), and Jim Gurley, Big Brother lead guitarist, at the Coffee Gallery, where they all perform on a semiregular basis.*

SPRING. Peter Albin and brother, Rodney, form their first band, the Liberty Hill Aristocrats—first gig at San Francisco Folk Festival.

SUMMER. Janis sings at Monterey Folk Festival, is involved in motorcycle accident, gets beaten up in a street brawl and is arrested for shoplifting.

FALL. Returns to San Francisco, performs on KPFA radio's Midnight Special.

1964   *SUMMER. Living in New York on Lower East Side. Reading Hesse and Nietzsche, shooting pool (and speed), occasionally singing at Slug's.*

Mug shot from 1963 shoplifting arrest

1965   *MAY Attempts (unsuccessfully) to get herself committed to San Francisco General Hospital.*
JUNE. Returns repentant and apparently reformed to Port Arthur. Registers in Sociology at Lamar Tech.
FALL. Sings at the Eleventh Door in Austin.
Meanwhile, back in San Francisco, Peter Albin and "Weird" Jim Gurley begin to assemble a band called Blue Yard Hill at 1090 Page Street. Begin playing at rent parties held in the basement, with newly recruited member Sam Andrew, a student at San Francisco State. Peter, Rodney, Chuck Jones (Big Brother's first drummer) and Chet Helms of the Family Dog, are all living in the huge Victorian house at 1090 Page, originally an Irish boarding house, owned by

Albin's parents. On weekends, Chet organizes jam session/dance parties in the basement. Sam Andrew (future guitar player with Big Brother) is a friend of someone who is now also hanging out at 1090 Page. Peter Albin has taught himself to play bass, and Paul Ferraz (a/k/a Beck), Big Brother's original manager, suggests putting an ad in the paper for a guitar player. David Erickson answers the ad and the group (Peter and Rodney Albin, Chuck Jones, Sam Andrew and David Erickson) start making up names for the band: Tom Swift and the Electric Grandmother, the Greenleaf Boys, the Acapulco Singers, etc. Two other possible names (Big Brother, the Holding Company) come up while playing Monopoly. They name the band after a combination of the two.

1090 Page Street. God's eye symbol (on button) was
Big Brother's logo

Peter announces the mission of Big Brother &
the Holding Company: "To speak to all the
children of the Earth." They play blues,
bluegrass, Rolling Stones style R&B, Dylan,
and folk/rock numbers like "I Know You,
Rider" in local bars and clubs. David
Erickson is under 21, which excludes them
from a number of gigs in places that have a
liquor license. He is eventually replaced as
drummer by Dave Getz, a teacher at the Art
Institute by day, and a waiter at the
Spaghetti Factory by night. Jim Gurley, who
knows Chet from the Family Dog house on
Page, begins dropping by to sit in on sessions.
Plays acoustic guitar with a mike stuck on it.
Gurley, known as "the fastest fingers in the
West," brings a decided touch of craziness to
the group with his concept of "freak rock," a
psychedelic synthesis of progressive jazz, raga

A pre-Janis, pre-Getz Big Brother with, from left to right, manager
Chet Helms, Sam Andrew, Peter Albin, Chuck Jones and Jim Gurley

riffs, hard rock and sound effects. In late '65 Big Brother makes their debut at a benefit for the Open Theater in Berkeley (again in the basement of 1090 Page).

1966   *JANUARY. Singing in Austin clubs—still mainly Bessie Smith and folk blues numbers. JANUARY 22. Big Brother plays their first official gig. Aided by Donald Buchla's synthesizer, they perform, along with the Grateful Dead, in the legendary first Trips Festival at the Longshoreman's Hall. Their repertoire consists of freak jazz—Sun Ra, Coltrane, Pharoah Sanders—R&B, music of the Mystic East and fuzz tone/feedback distortion.*
FEBRUARY 19. Big Brother play at the first "Tribal Stomp" at the Fillmore. This is drummer Chuck Jones's last gig with the group. He is replaced by Dave Getz. For the next four or five months they play Bay Area gigs. Of one of these, a San Francisco newspaperman says, "a quintet of Liverpool like singers and long hair and loud guitars." From their association with Chet Helms, who is now acting as their manager, the group has a regular weekend gig as the house band at the Avalon Ballroom (for which Chet books bands).
MARCH. At a benefit for Texas blues singer Teodar Jackson, Janis sings "Going to Brownsville," "I Ain't Got To Worry," and

Buffy St. Marie's "Codeine."
MAY. Considers joining Texas blues/rock group, the Thirteenth Floor Elevators. Chet and the band, seeing success of other bands with female lead singers (Jefferson Airplane with Signe Anderson and the Great Society with Grace Slick), consider adding a "chick singer" to the group. Chet suggests an old friend from his Austin days: Janis Joplin. Dispatches Travis Rivers, Janis's old high school friend from Port Arthur, to go to Texas and persuade her to come to San Francisco and try out as lead singer for Big Brother.
MAY 10. Janis leaves with Travis for San Francisco, by way of Austin.
JUNE 4. Arrive in San Francisco.
JUNE 10. Performs with Big Brother for the first time—at the Avalon Ballroom.
JUNE 19. St. Francis Hotel. Tim Leary Benefit.
JULY 1. Moves to a house in Lagunitas in the San Geronimo Valley with members of Big Brother, their wives and girlfriends.
JULY 17–18. The Avalon.
JULY 28. Performs at California Hall (on Cheaper Thrills).
Bob Shad, who owns Mainstream Records in Detroit, comes to San Francisco to audition bands. Wants to sign Big Brother, but Chet vetoes it.

OCTOBER 7–8. The Avalon.
OCTOBER 15–16. The Avalon.
NOVEMBER 1–6. The Matrix.
NOVEMBER 25–26. The Avalon.
DECEMBER 9–10. The Avalon.

1967   *JANUARY 1. Along with the Grateful Dead
and the Diggers' band, Orkustra, Big
Brother perform at the New Year's
Wail/Whale in Panhandle Park—The Hell's
Angels thank you party celebrating the bailing
out of Chocolate George by the Haight
Ashbury community.*
*JANUARY 14. Big Brother perform at the
first Be-In in Golden Gate Park. Also in
attendance: the Grateful Dead, Jefferson
Airplane, Sir Douglas Quintet, Loading
Zone, etc.*
JANUARY 17. The Matrix.
JANUARY 22. The Matrix.
*JANUARY 31. Matrix performance.
"Amazing Grace/High Heel Sneakers
Medley" (on* Farewell Song*).*

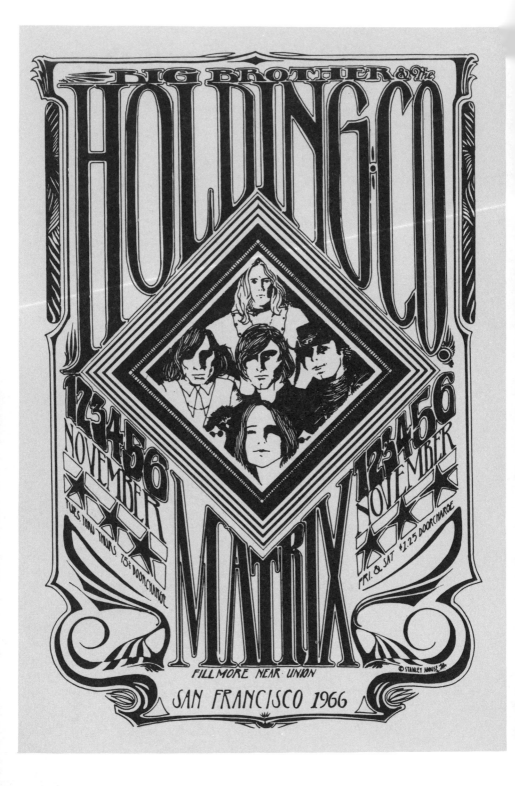

FEBRUARY 5. Performance at California Hall with Blue Cheer, sponsored by Hell's Angels as a benefit for Hairy Harry. Performance delayed while University of California law students finish bar exams.
FEBRUARY 10–11. At a concert at the Golden Sheaf Bakery in Berkeley, Janis meets Country Joe MacDonald, whose group, the Fish are also on the bill. Shortly afterwards, Janis moves in with Country Joe.
FEBRUARY 17–18. Second Annual Tribal Stomp, celebrating the first anniversary of the Family Dog, at the Avalon Ballrom. Quicksilver Messenger Service also on the bill. Chete Helms promises to provide "dance provocateurs" to incite audience participation.

*FEBRUARY 19. The Fillmore with
Jefferson Airplane.
FEBRUARY 24. Performs "Amazing
Grace" at the Invisible Circus/Rite of Spring
event for Glide Memorial Church. Michael
McClure, among others, participates.
MARCH 4. Performs with Steve Miller
Band in Journey to the End of Night event
at California Medical Center auditorium.
MARCH 17–18. Avalon Ballroom with Sir
Douglas Quintet and Charles Lloyd.
MARCH 31. The Avalon.
APRIL 1. The Avalon.
APRIL 11. The Fillmore.
APRIL 12–13. Winterland.*

APRIL 21–23. *The Fillmore.*
APRIL 25–26. *The Matrix.*
MAY 5–7. *Avalon with Sir Douglas Quintet and Orkustra.*
May 12–13. Winterland.
May 24–26. Carousel Ballroom with the Clara Ward Singers and H. P. Lovecraft. Poster by Stanley Mouse.
MAY 26–27. *The Fillmore.*
JUNE 2–3. *California Hall.*
JUNE 8–11. *The Avalon.*
JUNE 17. *First performance at Monterey Pop Festival, on Saturday afternoon, along with Canned Heat, Al Kooper, Steve Miller Band, Paul Butterfield Blues Band, Mike Bloomfield and the Electric Flag.*

BIG BROTHER & THE HOLDING COMPANY

PERSONAL MANAGEMENT: ABC/M INC./ALBERT B. GROSSMAN/JOHN COURT/75 E.55 ST., N.Y.C.

JUNE 18. Second performance of Big Brother added Sunday night so that they can be filmed for D. A. Pennebaker's Monterey Pop *along with the Byrds, Jimi Hendrix, the Who, the Mamas and Papas, and the Blues Project.*
JUNE 21. Big Brother perform at Summer Solstice celebrations in Golden Gate Park (with the Dead, Quicksilver Messenger Service, etc.), using equipment borrowed from Monterey Pop.
JUNE 24–25. The Avalon with Quicksilver Messenger Service.

JULY 31. Benefit for Free City. Blue Cheer, Charlatans (who), etc.

AUGUST 11. Digger Emmett Grogan announces trip. Big Sur, Portland, etc.

AUGUST 12-13. The Avalon.

AUGUST 25-27. The Avalon.

SEPTEMBER 8-9. Perform in Denver, Colorado.

SEPTEMBER 15. The Hollywood Bowl.

OCTOBER 5. Police close down the Matrix during Big Brother performance.

OCTOBER 7-8. Avalon with the Doors.

Big Brother in the Big Apple

JULY 31. Benefit for Free Clinic along with Blue Cheer, Charlatans (with Bill Cosby on drums), etc.
AUGUST 11. Digger Emmett Grogan announces travelling San Francisco tribal tour.
AUGUST 12–13. The Avalon.
AUGUST 25–27. The Avalon.
SEPTEMBER 8–9. Perform in Denver, Colorado.
SEPTEMBER 15. The Hollywood Bowl.
OCTOBER 6. Police close down the Matrix during Big Brother performance.
OCTOBER 7–8. Avalon with the Jim

Big Brother in the Big Apple

*JUNE 18. Second performance of Big
Brother added Sunday night so that they can
be filmed for D. A. Pennebaker's* Monterey
Pop *along with the Byrds, Jimi Hendrix, the
Who, the Mamas and Papas, and the Blues
Project.
JUNE 21. Big Brother perform at Summer
Solstice celebrations in Golden Gate Park
(with the Dead, Quicksilver Messenger
Service, etc.), using equipment borrowed
from Monterey Pop.
JUNE 24–25. The Avalon with Quicksilver
Messenger Service.*

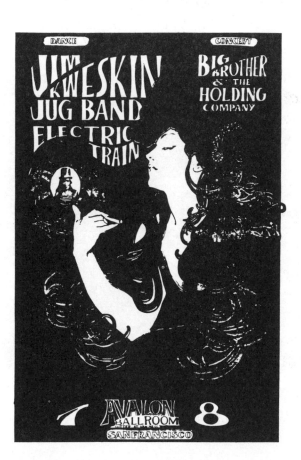

APRIL 21–23. The Fillmore.
APRIL 25–26. The Matrix.
MAY 5–7. Avalon with Sir Douglas Quintet
and Orkustra.
May 12–13. Winterland.
May 24–26. Carousel Ballroom with the
Clara Ward Singers and H. P. Lovecraft.
Poster by Stanley Mouse.
MAY 26–27. The Fillmore.
JUNE 2–3. California Hall.
JUNE 8–11. The Avalon.
JUNE 17. First performance at Monterey
Pop Festival, on Saturday afternoon, along
with Canned Heat, Al Kooper, Steve Miller
Band, Paul Butterfield Blues Band, Mike
Bloomfield and the Electric Flag.

BIG BROTHER & THE HOLDING COMPANY

PERSONAL MANAGEMENT: ABC/M INC./ALBERT B. GROSSMAN/JOHN COURT/75 E.55 ST.,N.Y.C.

A ZENEFIT

THE GRATEFUL DEAD
BIG BROTHER
AND THE HOLDING CO.
QUICKSILVER MESSENGER SERVICE
LUMINARIES BY BILL HAM
AVALON BALLROOM
SUTTER + VAN NESS / SAN FRANCISCO
NOV. 13TH SUN.
8PM-12PM
$2.00 TICKET AT DOOR
PLEASE COME...

· ZEN MOUNTAIN CENTER BENEFIT

Kweskin Jug Band and Electric Train.
OCTOBER 15–16. The Avalon.
OCTOBER 28–29. The Peacock Country
Club in San Raphael.
NOVEMBER 2. The Fillmore.
NOVEMBER 3–4. Winterland.
NOVEMBER 13. Avalon Zenefit for the Zen
Mountain Center (with the Dead and
Quicksilver).
NOVEMBER 23–24. Dance at California
Hall with the Friendly Stranger.
NOVEMBER 25. The Avalon.
NOVEMBER. Big Brother signs
management deal with Albert Grossman.
DECEMBER. Home to Port Arthur for
Christmas.
DECEMBER 29–31. Winterland.

Other 1967 appearances include clubs in
Seattle and Vancouver, Cheetah/Los Angeles,
Psychedelic Supermarket/Boston, Golden
Bear Club/Huntington Beach, Straight
Theater/San Francisco and Mother
Blues/Chicago.

1968

FEBRUARY 17. First New York
appearance. At the Anderson Theatre. Rave
reviews in the New York Times, Village
Voice, *etc. Sign with Columbia Records.*
FEBRUARY. Appearances in Boston,
Cambridge, Providence and Chicago.

MARCH 1. First attempts to "capture" Big Brother live at the Grande Ballroom in Detroit (on Janis Live *album).*
MARCH 8. Opens the Fillmore East.
MARCH-APRIL. Sessions for Cheap Thrills *at Columbia's Studio E in New York.*

The band now billed as "Janis Joplin and Big Brother & the Holding Company." Janis getting massive media attention. Big Brother feel Janis is on a "star trip,"

Above: album cover reject featuring Big Brother in a hippie tableau.
Opposite: R. Crumb's cartoon cover for *Cheap Thrills* incorporated
the God's eye symbol into its design.

treating them like a back up band. Others are telling Janis the band is terrible and that she ought to dump them.

APRIL 2. The New Generation in New York.

APRIL 10. The Anaheim Convention Center in Los Angeles.

APRIL 11. ABC–TV's Hollywood Palace.

APRIL 13. Winterland in San Francisco. Live recording on Farewell Song.

APRIL. Cheap Thrills sessions continue at Columbia's Hollywood studios.

MAY 12. San Francisco Valley State College.

JUNE. The group returns to New York for more sessions. By now there are over 200 reels of tape in the can, but producer John

Simon thinks none of it is of good enough quality to be released. Meanwhile, the orders are so huge that Cheap Thrills *is already certified gold. Columbia president Clive Davis insists the album be released immediately.*
JUNE 23. The Carousel Ballroom.
JUNE 24. The Avalon.
AUGUST. Performs at the Newport Folk Festival in Rhode Island.

      Cheap Thrills *released. Sells over a million copies in the first month of release (despite mixed reviews).*
AUGUST 3. The Fillmore East with the Staples Singers.
AUGUST 23. The Singer Bowl, New York.
AUGUST 30–SEPTEMBER 1. The Palace of Fine Arts Festival in San Francisco.
SEPTEMBER. Manager Albert Grossman

announces an "amicable split" between Janis and Big Brother.

OCTOBER. Janis now constantly seen with her symbol—a bottle of Southern Comfort. Has boosted the company's sales to such an extent that she "extorts" a lynx coat from them. "What a hustle! Can you imagine? Getting paid for passing out for two years!"

NOVEMBER. Plays the Aragon and Cheetah in Chicago.

NOVEMBER 15. Last East Coast performance with Big Brother at Hunter College in Manhattan.

NOVEMBER 20. Albert Grossman asks Mike Bloomfield and Nick Gravenites to help Janis put together a new band.

NOVEMBER 30. Big Brother perform in Vancouver, Canada.

DECEMBER 1. Big Brother's last performance, with the Family Dog in San Francisco.

DECEMBER 18–19. In San Francisco Bloomfield and Gravenites assemble and rehearse the new group. A long list of names proposed (Janis Joplin & the Joplinaires, the

*Janis Joplin Review, etc.) but band
eventually becomes the Kozmic Blues band.
DECEMBER 20. Kozmic Blues booked to
make first appearance at the Stax/Volt
"Yuletide Thing" in Memphis. Still
untogether, have frantic last minute
rehearsals at Studio B of Stax/Volt Records
in Memphis. That night they attend the
Stax/Volt Christmas party.
DECEMBER 21. Second on the bill with a
number of highly professional soul bands,
Kozmic Blues gets a cool reception at
Memphis's Mid South Coliseum.
   Other appearances include Cincinnati,
the NARM Convention/Puerto Rico, the
Electric Factory/Philadelphia, the University
of Buffalo Music Festival, the Electric
Theater and Kinetic Playground/Chicago, the*

*Kaleidoscope/Los Angeles, and the Avalon
and Fillmore/San Francisco.*

1969   *FEBRUARY 1. A sympathetic but damaging
review of their perfomance "Memphis
Debut," by Stanley Booth, appears in*
Rolling Stone.
*FEBRUARY 8. Albert Grossman books the
band for "the most obscure venue we could
find," Rindge, New Hampshire, for a
"sound test."*

Ted Strshensky takes a reading while Peter Albin twirls his
moustache. Winterland, 1968

(TP2) TAMPA, Fla. Nov. 20 — V FOR VICTORY — Rock star Janis Joplin and
her attorney, Herbert Goldburg, leave police headquarters after a prelim-
inary hearing on obscenity charges lodged against the 26-year-old singer
when she allegedly cursed police who interrupted her performance Sunday.
Miss Joplin said the V sing stood for victory, "not peace." (ST. PETERS-
BURG OUT)(AP Wirephoto)(ets51506rf)1969

FEBRUARY 9. "Preview" concert at Boston Music Hall.
FEBRUARY 11–12. Fillmore East concerts get mixed reaction.
MARCH 4. CBS–TV's 60 Minutes— *"Carnegie Hall for Children."*
MARCH 15. Devastating review of Fillmore concerts and interviews with Janis in Rolling Stone. *"Janis: The Judy Garland of Rock?" by Paul Nelson, is the cover story.*
MARCH 18. The Ed Sullivan Show.
MARCH 20–22. Winterland.
MARCH 23. The Fillmore West.
MARCH 24. Ralph Gleason, in the San Francisco Chronicle, *suggests that Janis should "go back to Big Brother, if they'll have her."*
APRIL–MAY. European tour.
APRIL 4–12. Frankfurt concert filmed by German television (on Janis *soundtrack album).*
APRIL 13–30. Appearances in Stockholm, Amsterdam, Copenhagen, and Paris.
APRIL 21. Albert Hall concert in London. Rave reviews in Disc, Melody Maker, Telegraph, *etc.*
JUNE. Sessions for Kozmic Blues *album begin in Columbia's Hollywood studios.*
JUNE 20–22. Appearances at Newport Festival, Rhode Island, Devonshire Downs, England, and in Northridge, California.
JULY 5. The Atlanta Pop Festival.

JULY 18. First appearance on Dick Cavett Show.

JULY 19. Forest Hills, New York.

AUGUST 3. Sings duet with Little Richard at the Atlantic City Pop Festival.

AUGUST 16. Woodstock Music and Art Fair in Bethel, New York. Sam Andrew gives last performance with the group. Replaced by John Till.

AUGUST 31. International Pop Festival in Lewisville, Texas.

SEPTEMBER. Janis's lawyer brings suit against ad agency for Janis Joplin "rip off" used in TV commercial.

SEPTEMBER 1. New Orleans Pop Festival at the Baton Rouge International Speedway in Prairieville, Louisiana.

SEPTEMBER 20. The Hollywood Bowl.

OCTOBER. Austin and Houston.

NOVEMBER. Kozmic Blues *released.*

NOVEMBER 16. Charged with two counts of using vulgar and obscene language on stage during Curtis Hall concert in Tampa.

NOVEMBER 23. Auditorium Hall in Chicago.

NOVEMBER 27. Sings with Tina Turner at Rolling Stones concert at Madison Square Garden.

NOVEMBER 29–DECEMBER 1. West Palm Beach Rock Festival.

DECEMBER. Appearance in Nashville. Moves into new house in Larkspur, California.

*DECEMBER 19–20. Madison Square
Garden concert. Joined on stage by Johnny
Winter and Paul Butterfield. Is
"romantically linked" with Joe Namath.*
    *Other appearances in 1969 include the
ABC-TV's* Tom Jones Show, *the Quaker
City Rock Festival/Philadelphia, the Civic
Center/Baltimore, ABC-TV's show* Music
Scene, *and the Toronto Pop
Festival/Canada.*

1970   *JANUARY. Kozmic Blues disbanded.
FEBRUARY. Flies to Rio, Brazil, for*

Kozmic Blues band on the Dick Cavett Show. From left to right: Luis Gasca, Terry Clements, Cornelius "Snooky" Flowers, Janis, Lonnie Castille, Brad Campbell and Sam Andrew

Carnival. Plans a long vacation to "get off drugs and dry out."
MARCH 4. Fined $200.00 in absentia on obscenity charges in Tampa.
MARCH 20. Announces from Rio that she is "going off into the jungle with a big bear of a man"—David Niehaus.
MARCH 28. Records "One Night Stand" with Paul Butterfield at Columbia's Studio D in Hollywood (on Farewell Song*).*
APRIL. Assembles third and last group, Full Tilt Boogie.

APRIL 2. Gets tattoos on her wrist and over her heart, "One for the boys."
APRIL 4. Reunion with Big Brother at the Fillmore West.
APRIL 12. Plays with Big Brother at Winterland (on Live*).*
MAY. Full Tilt play their first gig on the same bill with Big Brother and their new lead singer Nick Gravenites (recorded live for Be a Brother*) at a Hell's Angels dance at Pepperland in San Rafael. Also play the University of Florida at Gainesville, in Jacksonville, Florida, the Bar-B Ranch in Miami.*

Full Tilt Boogie. From left to right: Richard Bell, Ken Pearson, Brad Campbell, Clark Pierson and John Till

JUNE 12. Full Tilt play Freedom Hall in Louisville, Kentucky. Also play Kansas City, Santa Ana and San Bernardino.
JUNE 25. Dick Cavett Show.
JUNE 28–JULY 4. "Festival Express" tour across Canada (on Live*).*
JULY 8. Hawaiian concerts.
JULY 10. Sings at birthday celebration for Ken Threadgill in Austin.
JULY 11. Full Tilt and Big Brother share billing in San Diego.

With Eric Andersen in Winnipeg

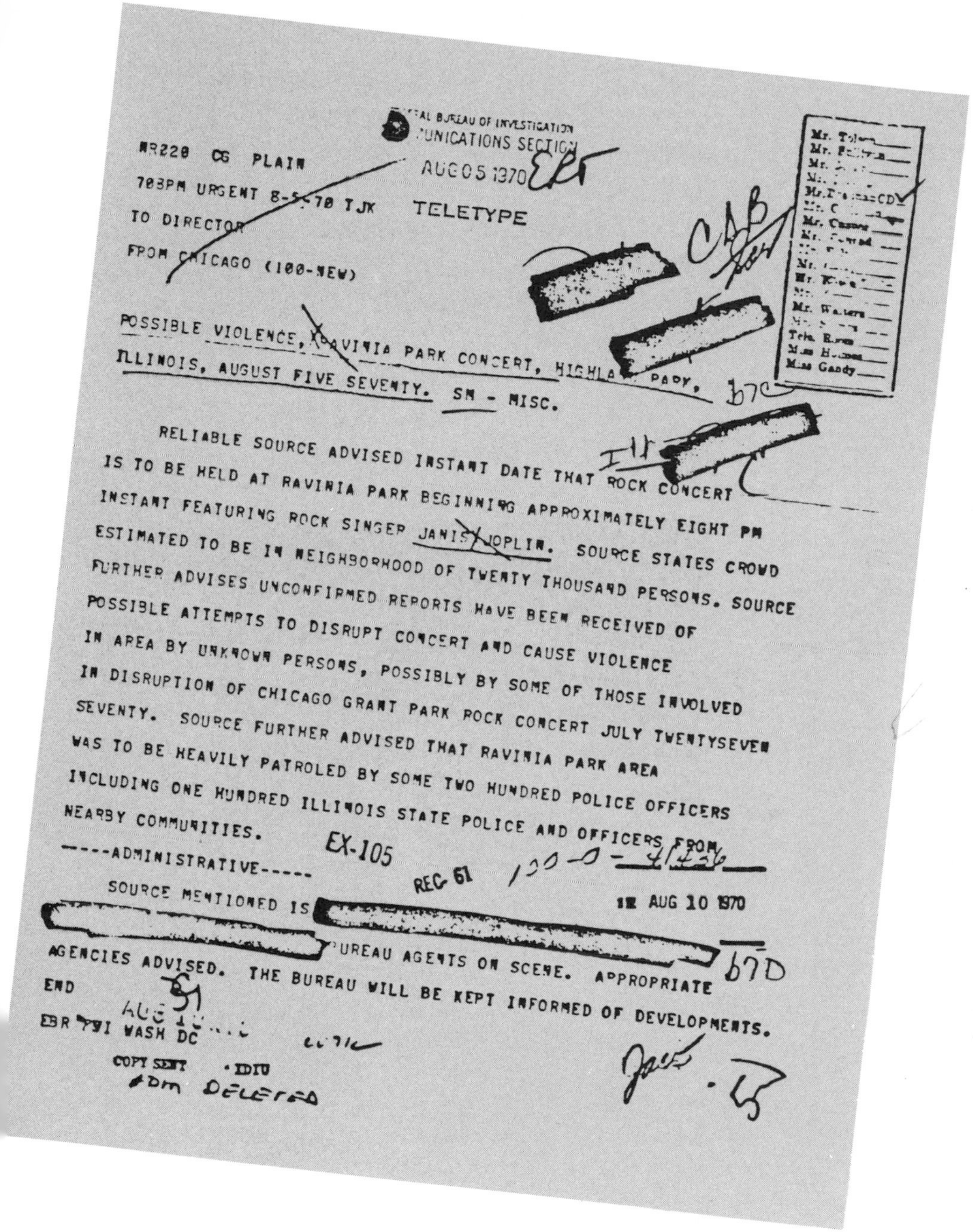

FEDERAL BUREAU OF INVESTIGATION
COMMUNICATIONS SECTION
AUG 05 1970
TELETYPE

NR228 CG PLAIN

703PM URGENT 8-5-70 TJK

TO DIRECTOR

FROM CHICAGO (100-NEW)

POSSIBLE VIOLENCE, RAVINIA PARK CONCERT, HIGHLA[redacted] PARK, ILLINOIS, AUGUST FIVE SEVENTY. SM - MISC.

[redacted]

b7C

RELIABLE SOURCE ADVISED INSTANT DATE THAT ROCK CONCERT IS TO BE HELD AT RAVINIA PARK BEGINNING APPROXIMATELY EIGHT PM INSTANT FEATURING ROCK SINGER JANIS JOPLIN. SOURCE STATES CROWD ESTIMATED TO BE IN NEIGHBORHOOD OF TWENTY THOUSAND PERSONS. SOURCE FURTHER ADVISES UNCONFIRMED REPORTS HAVE BEEN RECEIVED OF POSSIBLE ATTEMPTS TO DISRUPT CONCERT AND CAUSE VIOLENCE IN AREA BY UNKNOWN PERSONS, POSSIBLY BY SOME OF THOSE INVOLVED IN DISRUPTION OF CHICAGO GRANT PARK ROCK CONCERT JULY TWENTYSEVEN SEVENTY. SOURCE FURTHER ADVISED THAT RAVINIA PARK AREA WAS TO BE HEAVILY PATROLED BY SOME TWO HUNDRED POLICE OFFICERS INCLUDING ONE HUNDRED ILLINOIS STATE POLICE AND OFFICERS FROM NEARBY COMMUNITIES.

EX-105 REC 61

----ADMINISTRATIVE-----

SOURCE MENTIONED IS [redacted] BUREAU AGENTS ON SCENE. APPROPRIATE AGENCIES ADVISED. THE BUREAU WILL BE KEPT INFORMED OF DEVELOPMENTS.

AUG 10 1970

b7D

END

EBR FBI WASH DC

COPY SENT

ADM DELETED

The F.B.I. file on Janis, long known to exist, turned out to be a single page about possible disturbances at a concert outside Chicago

AUGUST 1–2. Forest Hills, New York.
AUGUST 3. Last appearance on Dick
Cavett *(with Raquel Welch and Chet
Huntley).*
*AUGUST 4. Performance in Ravinia,
Illinois.*
*AUGUST 6. Performance at Shea Stadium
Peace Festival.*
*AUGUST 8. Performance at the Capitol
Theater in Port Chester, New York.*
*AUGUST 12. Gives last performance, at
Harvard Stadium.*
AUGUST 13. Flies to Port Arthur.
AUGUST 14. Attends high school reunion.
SEPTEMBER. Pearl *sessions in Los
Angeles.*
*OCTOBER 3. Janis listens to instrumental
of final track scheduled for* Pearl: *Nick
Gravenites's "Buried Alive In The Blues."
She plans to record vocal the following day.*
*OCTOBER 4. At 1:40 a.m., alone in her
room at the Landmark Hotel, Janis O.D.s
from a combination of heroin and alcohol.*

Other titles of interest

**THE ACCIDENTAL
EVOLUTION OF
ROCK'N'ROLL
A Misguided Tour Through
Popular Music**
Chuck Eddy
430 pp., 101 illus.
80741-6 $15.95

**ARE YOU EXPERIENCED?
The Inside Story of the
Jimi Hendrix Experience**
Noel Redding and Carol Appleby
258 pp., 28 photos
80681-9 $14.95

**THE DARK STUFF
Selected Writings on Rock Music,
1972–1995**
Nick Kent
Foreword by Iggy Pop
365 pp.
80646-0 $14.95

**DARK HORSE
The Life and Art of
George Harrison
Updated Edition**
Geoffrey Giuliano
395 pp., over 100 photos and illus.
80747-5 $14.95

**NO DIRECTION HOME
The Life and Music of Bob Dylan**
Robert Shelton
573 pp., 28 photos
80782-3 $17.95

**PINK FLOYD
through the eyes of . . . the band,
its fans, friends and foes**
Edited by Bruno MacDonald
400 pp., over two dozen photos
80780-7 $14.95

**BLACKBIRD
The Life and Times of
Paul McCartney
Updated Edition**
Geoffrey Giuliano
488 pp., over 90 photos
80781-5 $15.95

**STONE ALONE
The Story of a Rock 'n' Roll Band**
Bill Wyman with Ray Coleman
640 pp., 63 illus.
80783-1 $17.95

HEROES AND VILLAINS
The True Story of the Beach Boys
Steven Gaines
432 pp., 66 photos
80647-9 $14.95

THE LIFE AND TIMES OF
LITTLE RICHARD
Updated Edition
Charles White
337 pp., 70 photos
80552-9 $13.95

NO COMMERCIAL POTENTIAL
The Saga of Frank Zappa
Updated Edition
David Walley
240 pp., 28 photos
80710-6 $13.95

STRANDED
Rock and Roll for a Desert Island
Edited and with a new preface by
Greil Marcus
New foreword by
Robert Christgau
320 pp.
80682-7 $14.95

ERIC CLAPTON
Lost in the Blues
Updated Edition
Harry Shapiro
256 pp., 50 photos
80480-8 $14.95

BOB DYLAN: THE EARLY
YEARS
A Retrospective
Edited by Craig McGregor
New preface by Nat Hentoff
424 pp., 15 illus.
80416-6 $13.95

DIVIDED SOUL
The Life of Marvin Gaye
David Ritz
367 pp., 47 photos
80443-3 $13.95

ROCK ALBUMS OF THE 70s
A Critical Guide
Robert Christgau
480 pp.
80409-3 $16.95

Available at your bookstore

OR ORDER DIRECTLY FROM

DA CAPO PRESS

1-800-321-0050